Working with Aggression and Resistance in Social Work

Working with Aggression and Resistance in Social Work

Edited by
BRIAN J TAYLOR

Series Editors: Jonathan Parker and Greta Bradley

LearningMatters

© 2011 Gerry Heery (chapter 4), Campbell Killick (chapter 5), Trevor Lindsay (chapter 8), Roger Manktelow (chapter 7), James Marshall (chapter 6), Mary McColgan and Geraldine Fleming (chapter 9), Aisling Monds-Watson (chapter 2), Brian J Taylor (Introduction, chapter 3, Conclusion)

British Library Cataloguing in Publication Data
A CIP record for this book is available from the British Library

ISBN 978 0 85725 429 0

This book is also available in the following formats:
Adobe ebook ISBN: 978 0 85725 431 3
EPUB ebook ISBN: 978 0 85725 430 6
Kindle ISBN: 978 0 85725 432 0

The right of Gerry Heery (chapter 4), Campbell Killick (chapter 5), Trevor Lindsay (chapter 8), Roger Manktelow (chapter 7), James Marshall (chapter 6), Mary McColgan and Geraldine Fleming (chapter 9), Aisling Monds-Watson (chapters 1 and 2), Brian J Taylor (Introduction, chapter 3, Conclusion) to be identified as the Authors of this Work has been asserted by them in accordance with the Copyright, Designs and Patents Act 1988.

Cover and text design by Code 5 Design Associates Ltd
Project Management by Deer Park Productions
Typeset by Pantek Arts Ltd, Maidstone, Kent
Printed and bound in Great Britain by Bell & Bain Ltd, Glasgow

Learning Matters Ltd
20 Cathedral Yard
Exeter EX1 1HB
01392 215560
info@learningmatters.co.uk
www.learningmatters.co.uk

MIX
Paper from
responsible sources
FSC® C007785

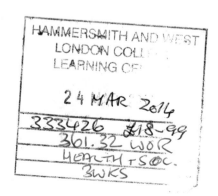

Contents

Editor and Contributors

Professor Mary McColgan is Professor of Social Work at the University of Ulster and Head of the School of Sociology and Applied Social Studies. She is a qualified social worker and practice teacher with a background in family and child care, and in healthcare practice. She has been involved with social work education and training for over 25 years and her research interests include child protection, family support and women's emotional health and well-being.

Geraldine Fleming is Commissioning Lead for Mental Health at the Health and Social Care Board for Northern Ireland, having previously been Assistant Director for Physical Health and Disability Services in the Northern Health and Social Care Trust. She is a qualified social worker with 15 years' experience working in adult social care. Her research interests include adult safeguarding, risk management and quality of services in adult care.

Gerry Heery is an independent social worker, trainer and consultant with over 25 years' experience in child care and justice work. He has been involved in developing and delivering domestic, family and general violence-related programmes and is author of *Preventing Violence in Relationships* (2000), the *Parents' Anger Management Programme* (2007) and the soon-to-be-published *Choosing Non-Violence: A Programme for Young People to Address the Use of Violence*. He lives with his wife Maire in Belfast and they have five children.

Dr Campbell Killick is Senior Social Worker (Research) with the South Eastern Health and Social Care Trust in Northern Ireland. His work focuses on enabling social workers to make use of best evidence in their practice and on developing research to inform social care services. He has had a lead role in training social work staff in adult protection work, and he has been involved in a number of studies relating to the protection of vulnerable adults from abuse.

Trevor Lindsay is Lecturer in Social Work at the University of Ulster with 17 years' experience in higher education. He draws on 20 years' probation practice specialising in groupwork and group care. He is the lead author of *Groupwork Practice in Social Work* and is editor and main contributor to *Social Work Interventions*, both in the Learning Matters Transforming Social Work Practice series.

Dr Roger Manktelow worked as a mental health social worker for some 15 years before moving to the University of Ulster at Magee where he has taught social work and mental health for the last 20 years. He has published widely in his research areas, which include statutory mental health social work, help-seeking in mental health, mental health inequalities, and the mental health needs of the victims of the Northern Ireland troubles.

James Marshall is Associate Lecturer at the University of Ulster and an independent social worker with 25 years' experience in family and child care practice. He teaches undergraduate and postgraduate child care and has recently written a social work guide for the Health and Social Care Board on child care practice in Northern Ireland. His research area is child protection practice, in particular investigative interviewing of children for court.

Aisling Monds-Watson is Lecturer in Social Work at the University of Ulster, having previously practised in both community mental health, and in family and child care social work. Her research is in the area of adult mental health, with a particular focus on social work with mothers experiencing mental health difficulties.

Dr Brian J Taylor is Senior Lecturer in Social Work at the University of Ulster, having previously spent 12 years as a social work practitioner and manager and 15 years in employer-based training and development. He has faced aggression and violence as a social work practitioner and has known colleagues and students who have been assaulted by clients during his 30 years in the profession. He is accredited as a Personal Safety Advisor with the British Judo Association and has trained with the Care and Responsibility personal safety framework for health and social care staff.

Series Editors' Preface

The Western world including the UK face numerous challenges over forthcoming years. These include dealing with the impact of an increasingly ageing population, with its attendant social care needs and working with the financial implications that such a changing demography brings. At the other end of the life-span the need for high quality child care, welfare and safeguarding services have been highlighted as society develops and responds to a changing complexion.

Migration has developed as a global phenomenon and we now live and work with the implications of international issues in our everyday and local lives. Often these issues influence how we construct our social services and determine what services we need to offer. It is likely that as a social worker you will work with a diverse range of people throughout your career, many of whom have experienced significant, even traumatic, events that require a professional and caring response. As well as working with individuals, however, you may be required to respond to the needs of a particular community disadvantaged by world events or excluded within local communities because of assumptions made about them. What is clear within these contexts is that you may be working with a range of people who would, to say the least, rather not be involved with social workers, or may be actively aggressive and violent. This book provides important knowledge and information to help you become aware of these issues, to protect yourself and respond appropriately when faced with potential violence.

The importance of social work education came to the fore again following the inquiry into the death of baby Peter and the subsequent report from the Social Work Task Force set up in its aftermath. It is timely, also, to reconsider elements of social work education as is being taken forward by the Reform Board process in England – indeed, we should view this as a continual striving for excellence! Reflection, revision and reform allow us to focus clearly on what knowledge is useful to engage with in learning to be a social worker. The focus on 'statutory' social work, and by dint of that involuntary clients, brings issues of non-cooperation and aggression to the fore. This important book provides readers with a beginning sense of the realities of practice and the importance of safe practice.

The books in this series respond to the agendas driven by changes brought about by professional body, Government and disciplinary review. They aim to build on, and offer, introductory texts based on up to date knowledge and to help communicate this in an accessible way, preparing the ground for future study as you develop your social work career. The books are written by people passionate about social work and social services and aim to instil that passion on others. The knowledge introduced in this book is important for all social workers in all fields of practice as they seek to reaffirm social work's commitment to those it serves.

Professor Jonathan Parker, Bournemouth University
Greta Bradley, University of York

Acknowledgements

The writing team would like to acknowledge the support of our students and colleagues at the University of Ulster and in the health and social care employing bodies in Northern Ireland with whom we have shared ideas and from whom we have learnt so much. We are grateful for the advice of the Series Editor, Professor Jonathan Parker, and of Luke Block and Kate Lodge at Learning Matters. We would particularly like to thank Lauren Gregg who painstakingly tidied up the presentation of the text.

This book is dedicated to all social workers who continue to do their best to serve clients and families despite the limited thanks they sometimes receive from some of the media at the present time.

Introduction

Brian J Taylor

This book has been written to address the need among students on qualifying social work professional training to develop the knowledge and skills to work with clients and families who are less than enthusiastic about the help and support offered, and those who may be aggressive. It cannot give a blueprint, but gives helpful pointers to aid the reader's understanding of involuntary interactions and reflection on their developing practice.

Ambivalent clients and families

Numerically the majority of social work clients are older people and those with disabilities and health problems who are grateful for the help and support given, particularly at times of crisis and life-changing decisions about care. However, social work frequently involves working with more reluctant clients.

Child protection work involves a safeguarding role on behalf of society as well as offering support to families identified as most in need. Those alleged or suspected of abuse or neglect are unlikely to take kindly to assessment or intervention by professionals – most often led or co-ordinated by a social worker. Nor can a warm welcome be assumed by a child who may well fear being removed from home despite any harm that has been inflicted by family members. Despite earnest desires to help families to improve established patterns of living and relating, engaging in a helping process with an outsider, even though professional, can be experienced as too embarrassing.

The growing field of adult protection work involves a safeguarding as well as supportive helping role, even if there is not the same mandate for compulsory intervention as there is with children. Convicted offenders may distrust anyone in an authority role, quite apart from the possibility of feeling envious of someone who has a job and is making their way honestly in society. Drug users may be reserved with you because of your role and duties in relation to possible prosecution. Older people and those in palliative care, hospital and primary health care settings may not be clear about the social work role or may consider you too young or inexperienced to be able to help. Work in mental health, dementia and learning disability involves some who may harm themselves or others, including you as a social worker, even though you are trying to enable them to achieve a fulfilling life and overcome some of life's challenges. People with physical disability and sensory impairments may question whether you are knowledgeable enough about their health and technical aspects of their circumstances to be able to help. In some instances there may be deep-seated anger arising from their disability or the hurt felt from prejudiced or unthinking attitudes that they encounter. Such pain may come to the surface at a time of personal helping by a social worker.

Prevalence of aggression towards social workers

There are a number of contexts of social work practice where high numbers of assaults are reported. This includes day care facilities for people with learning disability, children's homes and psychiatric hospitals. However, assaults occur in every field of practice including field social work with all client groups, and in residential, supportive housing and day support settings of every variety. The *Social work task force report* in the UK (Department for Children, Schools and Families, 2009) highlights that the knowledge and skills required to work with conflict and hostility is an area that is not being covered in sufficient depth on some qualifying social work programmes. This book has been written to help to address that need.

RESEARCH SUMMARY

Estimated percentage of staff suffering one or more assaults at work during the past year by occupational grouping

- *Health and social welfare professionals (incl. nurses and social workers)*   *3.3%*
- *Protective service occupations (incl. prison officers and doormen)*   *2.6%*
- *Transport and mobile machine drivers and operatives*   *1.9%*
- *Managers and proprietors – services and agriculture*   *1.8%*
- *Medical, dental and psychology professions*   *1.4%*
- *Caring personal service occupations*   *1.3%*
- *Leisure and other personal service occupations*   *1.1%*
- *Teaching and research professions*   *1.0%*

(Upson, 2004, based on data from the British Crime Survey)

Employer and employee responsibilities

In the United Kingdom employers have a statutory obligation to identify the nature and extent of risk to their employees and visitors to their premises, and to devise measures to provide safe systems of work. The current underpinning statute in Great Britain is the Health and Safety at Work Act 1974, and in Northern Ireland the Health and Safety at Work (NI) Order 1978, both of which have been subsequently amended. The Health and Safety Executives established under this statute aim to *reduce work-related death and serious injury in workplaces* (www.hse.gov.uk/aboutus/index.htm).

In discharging these responsibilities, the Health Services Advisory Commission of the Health and Safety Executive for England recommended (1987) that employers should:

• provide suitable training including in the physical management of aggression;

• develop effective policies;

• develop support systems for staff subjected to assault or aggressive behaviour.

It is beyond the scope of this book to look at the responsibilities of employers to implement their statutory responsibilities and recommendations such as these. Environmental factors may influence the likelihood of assault. It is also beyond the scope of this book to consider the design of for example interview rooms or waiting areas, which are the responsibility of employers (Bibby, 1994, chapter 10) although you should contribute your views on such issues as appropriate as a professional engaged in social work.

The focus of this book is on the development of skills by beginning social workers across a range of settings. The aim is to establish a solid foundation for confident professional practice, upon which specialist skills may be built. It is important that you as a professional have support from your employer as to what represents acceptable practice in avoiding assault – to yourself, to other staff and to other clients in group care settings. Uncertainty about employer support can lead to greater anxiety and hesitation during incidents, thereby increasing the likelihood of assault. Within your own role you should use appropriate channels to convey your training needs and your concerns about any substantial perceived lack in policies, systems and arrangements to protect you from assault and aggression.

Caveats

This book gives you some ideas to help you to reflect on your practice and instinctive reactions to challenging situations. In any particular situation only you can decide what action to take to try to avoid assault, defuse aggression or seek to engage a reluctant client or family. Not all ideas will work for all people in every situation. Despite the efforts of individuals and employers, on some occasions professionals are injured by clients. These ideas are to prompt your thinking about how to engage those who are resistant, respond to difficult situations so as to reduce the likelihood and seriousness of assault and achieve the best possible outcome in the circumstances for the client, family and others in society. This book cannot address your need to learn physical skills for breaking away from being held, and for team restraint in certain settings. These cannot be learned from a book and must be practised so as to develop 'muscle memory', not just head knowledge. You should seek training from your employer on this as a priority.

In this book any reference to legal matters is intended only as an introductory guide for general education by non-lawyers for non-lawyers. Do not rely upon this book as a substitute for legal advice on any individual set of circumstances. This book aims to inform you about general principles and issues so that you are more able to identify when legal advice needs to be sought, and enable you to better understand and discuss the issues. This book does not purport to address the detailed legal requirements in any particular jurisdiction, but to educate on general principles that are common in democratic countries.

Structure of this book

We have tried to give coherence to chapters by running a case study about the same family throughout the book, as this approach seems to have been very well received in an earlier book by some of the same team of authors (Lindsay, 2009). The earlier chapters in this book lay a foundation for later chapters by considering definitions of terms (Chapter 1), theories of aggression (Chapter 2) (both by Aisling Monds-Watson) and general principles for avoiding assault and defusing aggressive situations (Chapter 3). In Chapter 4 Gerry Heery considers the challenges of the developing field of work now conceptualised as domestic violence, which has relevance to social work with families across client groups. This chapter highlights the complexity of family relationships and the challenges in engaging resistant family members. The following chapters consider the issues of ambivalence and aggression in relation to particular client groups each with their own types of needs. In Chapter 5 Campbell Killick discusses approaches to engaging reluctant victims of adult abuse and the alleged perpetrators. James Marshall, in Chapter 6, addresses issues in engaging families as part of child protection social work, not least so as to protect children from harm while reducing the need to take them into state care. In Chapter 7 Roger Manktelow discusses the challenges of irrationality in mental health social work and the pointers that might indicate dangerousness. Trevor Lindsay, in Chapter 8, outlines practical approaches to managing conflict and resistance in group work in various settings so as to seek beneficial therapeutic outcomes. Chapter 9, by Mary McColgan and Geraldine Fleming, focuses on the challenges inherent in the social work role as care manager, when less than satisfactory practice in social care services must be addressed, frequently in the context of resistance from the service providers.

Chapters follow the model adopted by Learning Matters of relating the chapters to the relevant National Occupational Standards, and include plentiful illustrative material such as research summaries and activities to aid learning. As with other books in the series, you are encouraged to work through the book as an active participant. Such interactive learning will help in developing an understanding of the material that is integrated with your values and other knowledge and skills. In this way it is more readily transferred to skills that you can use readily as required. Reflective practice – reflecting on your practice in the light of research, theory, law, principles, policy and standards – is at the heart of professional development.

National Occupational Standards

This book will help you to develop the professional skills necessary to meet the National Occupational Standards for Social Work in the UK including the following.

Key Role 1: Prepare for, and work with individuals, families, carers, groups and communities to assess their needs and circumstances.

• Prepare for social work contact and involvement.

Key Role 2: Plan, carry out, review and evaluate social work practice, with individuals, families, carers, groups, communities and other professionals.

- Respond to crisis situations.

- Interact with individuals, families, carers, groups and communities to achieve change and development and to improve life opportunities.

- Address behaviour which presents a risk to individuals, families, carers, groups and communities.

Key Role 4: Manage risk to individuals, families, carers, groups, communities, self and colleagues.

- Assess and manage risks to individuals, families, carers, groups and communities.

- Assess, minimise and manage risk to self and colleagues.

Key Role 6: Demonstrate professional competence in social work practice.

- Work within agreed standards of social work practice and ensure own professional development.

This book will help you to gain some of the knowledge required for professional social work practice and achieve the academic standards as set out in the 2008 Subject Benchmark Statement for Social Work of the Quality Assurance Agency for Higher Education in the UK including the following.

3.1.4 Social work theory

- Models and methods of assessment, including factors underpinning the selection and testing of relevant information, the nature of professional judgement and the process of risk assessment.

3.1.5 The nature of social work practice

- The nature and characteristics of skills associated with effective practice, both direct and indirect, with a range of service users and in a variety of settings, including group care.

- The relevance of psychological and physiological perspectives to understanding individual and social development and functioning.

5.5.4 Intervention and evaluation

- Build and sustain purposeful relationships with people and organisations in community-based and inter-professional contexts, including group care.

- Undertake practice in a manner that promotes well-being and protects the safety of all parties.

5.6 Communication skills

- Use both verbal and non-verbal cues to guide interpretation.

5.8 Skill in personal and professional development

• Handle interpersonal and intrapersonal conflict constructively.

See appendix p135 for the subject Benchmark for Social Work.

Terminology

Key terms such as 'ambivalence', 'aggression', 'violence' and 'hostility' are defined in Chapter 1.

Some social workers in the UK prefer the term 'service user' to 'client'. The best evidence available suggests that this is not a preference of people who come into contact with social workers professionally (Lloyd et al., 2001; Keaney et al., 2004; Covell et al., 2007; McKeown, 2008). It may be that the current vogue for the term 'service user' in the UK is driven by politicians rather than by people who come into contact with social workers (Heffernan, 2006). The traditional and international term 'client', used widely to convey a professional supportive relationship in diverse fields such as business, law, finance and other human service professions, seems to convey the responsibility of the social worker for his or her actions (see Seal, 2008, p ix, in the context of supported living and housing services) and is widely preferred by those who come to social workers for help. The professional relationship, where the social worker contributes a particular area of knowledge and skills within an ethical framework, remains at the heart of effective social work practice. The client still makes the ultimate decision about treatment or action, as in other professional relationships, unless there is a safeguarding mandate from society. Many are put off the use of the term 'service user' because of the connotations of suggesting that people are exploiting services. We have had a very negative reaction to the term 'service user' from one of the people qualified by experience to advise us on our training programmes. The abbreviation 'user' has received a strong negative reaction locally from people who have experience of coming to social workers for help, because of the colloquial use of this term for people abusing drugs. In this text the authors of individual chapters have chosen their preferred terminology based on their experience in that field of practice, including terms such as 'client', 'patient', 'survivor', 'tenant', 'resident', and 'service user', although generally the term 'client' is used for the above reasons.

Conclusion

This book has been developed specifically for social workers undertaking qualifying professional social work study. It has been developed from the practice experience and teaching of the authors over decades. This book is to support you in that crucial process of undertaking your professional role and task effectively and safely despite resistance and aggression. Despite the challenges, remember that the service we offer is for the ultimate benefit of clients, families and the wider society.

Chapter 1

Defining key concepts: Aggression, ambivalence and resistance

Aisling Monds-Watson

ACHIEVING A SOCIAL WORK DEGREE

This chapter will help you to meet the following National Occupational Standards for Social Work in the UK including the following.

Key Role 1: Prepare for, and work with individuals, families, carers, groups and communities to assess their needs and circumstances.

Key Role 2: Plan, carry out, review and evaluate social work practice, with individuals, families, carers, groups, communities and other professionals.

- Interact with individuals, families, carers, groups and communities to achieve change and development and to improve life opportunities.
- Develop and maintain relationships with individuals, families, carers, groups, communities and others.
- Work with individuals, families, carers, groups, communities and others to avoid crisis situations and address problems.
- Apply and justify social work methods and models used to achieve change and development, and to improve life opportunities.
- Work with individuals, families, carers, groups, communities and others to identify and evaluate situations and circumstances that may trigger the behaviour.
- Work with individuals, families, carers, groups and communities on strategies and support that could positively change the behaviour.

Key Role 3: Support individuals to represent their needs, views and circumstances.

Key Role 4: Manage risk to individuals, families, carers, groups, communities, self and colleagues.

Key Role 6: Demonstrate professional competence in social work practice.

It will also introduce you to the following academic standards as set out in the 2008 social work subject benchmark statement.

5.1.3 Values and ethics.
5.1.4 Social work theory.
5.5.3 Analysis and synthesis.
5.6 Communication skills.
5.8 Skill in personal and professional development.

Introduction

When the social anthropologist Catherine Lutz (1988) researched the remote Micronesian Ifaluk people in the late twentieth century, she discovered they had five different words for anger. *Nguch* referred to the anger experienced when a friend or family member had let you down; *tipmochmoch* was the bad temper and irritability experienced when tired or convalescing from illness and *tang* described the anger experienced when feeling helpless or trapped into unwelcome commitments. Anger which results from the culmination of a series of negative experiences was called *lingeringer*, and moral anger in response to injustice was known as *song*.

Lutz theorised that because the Ifaluk people distinguished between different types of anger and regarded each as a discrete and individual emotion, they were able to be more sensitive to each other's emotional states, and manage and respond to anger in a more intelligent and empathetic manner.

Lutz's theory about the Ifaluk people is similar to the relatively recent notion of emotional intelligence, which David Howe (2008, p12) neatly summarises as *the ability to understand both ourselves and other people as emotional beings*. However, this sounds deceptively simple. An aptitude for emotional intelligence depends on multiple factors:

> *the capacity to reason about emotions, and of emotions to enhance thinking ... the abilities to accurately perceive emotions, to access and generate emotions so as to assist thought, to understand emotions and emotional knowledge, and to reflectively regulate emotions so as to promote emotional and intellectual growth.*

> (Mayer et al., 2004, p197)

This book aims to increase the emotional intelligence of its readers by offering knowledge and understanding of the more challenging emotional states likely to be both encountered and experienced by social workers, so that like the Ifaluk, we too can manage and respond in a sensitive, intelligent and empathetic fashion.

Social work practice is routinely undertaken with service users during the most traumatic and challenging periods of their lives, when they are subject to high degrees of social, emotional and environmental stress. Service users are also likely to have experienced levels of adversity, discrimination, oppression or disadvantage, which may have led them to acquire behaviours that create barriers to therapeutic or productive work. Alternatively they may have developed ways of managing their feelings which make it difficult for you as a social worker to engage with them. They may also be experiencing high levels of emotions which they have difficulty containing, and which are expressed in actions that are threatening, intimidating, frightening or which present an actual risk of physical or emotional harm.

Working with service users who display challenging behaviours for a variety of reasons and in a variety of contexts is a common aspect of social work practice. Therefore it is vital that social workers have the knowledge to practise ethically, safely and effectively in these situations. This requires a clear understanding of:

- the definitions and terms used to label and describe challenging behaviours;

- the most relevant theoretical explanations to help understand and anticipate challenging behaviours;

- the practical skills required to deal with challenging behaviours in various practice settings.

This chapter will examine and clarify the terms used to label and describe a range of challenging behaviours you are likely to encounter in practice. Some of these labels are attached to behaviours (such as aggression and violence), and some refer to feelings (such as anger and ambivalence). These are things that are sometimes easier to describe than define, so some time will be spent illustrating these concepts and offering commonly accepted definitions. The chapter will begin by looking at anger, aggression, hostility and violence, before exploring the concepts of ambivalence and resistance. The following case study about Mary, Jim and family will be used to illustrate the various terms, and will be referred to in subsequent chapters to exemplify some of the theories and interventions applicable to working in situations characterised by aggression and/or resistance.

CASE STUDY

Mary (46) and Jim (54) have three children: their sons Frank (2 years old) and Tom (15 years old), and their daughter Alice (12 years old). Mary has a part-time job as a care assistant in a home for older people near where they live. Jim had been employed as a sheet metal worker since leaving school at 16. Jim enjoyed his work; he was an active union member, an industrious employee and had attained a senior position on the factory floor. He was also both popular and well respected by his workmates with whom he often socialised outside work. Unfortunately Jim was made redundant 18 months ago when the factory went out of business, and has been unemployed since.

Initially Jim enjoyed his redundancy; he thought it was a temporary setback and was optimistic that he would soon find another job. The redundancy package was generous and both Jim and Mary were pleased to be able to afford a family holiday and still have some money left over. Jim enjoyed having time to catch up with DIY in the home and the company of his friends, many of whom had also been made redundant. However, Jim has now been actively seeking work for 14 months without success, the firms he has approached prefer to take on 'school leavers' as apprentices at a minimum wage, and he has been told that his skills and training are 'out of date'.

Mary is now the primary wage earner and the family are struggling financially. Mary is hoping that she will be offered full-time work in the care home, before Jim's redundancy package runs out.

ACTIVITY **1.1**

Jim and his family are facing a difficult situation which is challenging them on personal, social, financial and emotional levels. The status quo within the home has shifted, and potential changes in Jim's sense of who he is, what he does, and how he feels are likely to be having far-reaching consequences for the entire family. Consider how Jim might be feeling at this point in his life. How might redundancy be threatening his sense of self worth? Make a list of all the things that Jim might feel he has lost along with his job.

COMMENT

It is important to integrate new knowledge with what you already know, and to understand theoretical ideas that you have been considering in the light of practical situations such as this one. Consciously make connections between social processes faced by clients and concepts from human growth and development.

What do the terms anger, aggression, hostility and violence actually mean?

Anger

Anger is a normal human emotion, which is experienced by everyone to varying degrees in varying circumstances. It serves multiple objectives, and is a motivating drive which can energise us to challenge injustice, change our behaviours, adjust our lifestyle, or protect ourselves and others. Defined by the *Oxford English Dictionary* as *a strong feeling of annoyance, displeasure, or hostility*, anger is an unpleasant feeling to which we can all relate. But how much do we really know about anger and what makes it different to hostility and aggression?

Various theories exist which try to explain why we experience anger, and we shall explore these in detail in Chapter 2. For now we will look at the origins, physiological effects and expression of anger.

During the 1960s and 1970s the social anthropologist Paul Ekman (2004) undertook research into the facial expression of emotion, to try to establish that emotions were expressed differently in different cultures. Most scientists at this time believed that the facial expression of emotion was learnt, and therefore culturally unique. Ekman showed pictures of different facial expressions to tribesmen in Papua New Guinea and other culturally diverse locations. However, instead of confirming that emotional expression was culturally specific, Ekman established that six basic emotions were universally recognisable: anger, fear, sadness, surprise, disgust and joy. This implied that the expression of these emotions was biological rather than socially conditioned, and that humankind had evolved to collectively express and recognise these primary emotions for very specific reasons.

Humanity's shared evolutionary history means that all human bodies are alike, and so too are all human minds; Dylan Evans (2001, p10) calls this the *psychological unity of humankind*. Not only are the six basic emotions universal, they are also instinctual and innate biological responses over which we have little conscious control. This means that we are hard-wired to respond to certain stimuli in certain ways. Our brains automatically appraise our experiences as they occur and create emotional responses to correspond with that unconscious appraisal. This means that these emotional responses occur without us having thought about them. Paul Ekman (2004) talks about *autoappraisers*, the automatic appraisal mechanisms which occur unconsciously in response to visual, auditory and sensory triggers, and create the physiological responses we call emotions. Basically this means that when confronted by something which we find threatening, humans unconsciously respond in particular physical and emotional ways. The sensations we experience as anger are the physiological preparations the body makes in order to protect itself.

ACTIVITY 1.2

Think about occasions when you've felt angry. What provoked your anger? How did your body feel? What did you do? What were you unable to do? What would have helped you to manage how you were feeling? What would have made you feel worse?

Think about a time when you were with someone who was angry. How did their anger make you feel? Did you want to be there?

COMMENT

When we feel angry our heart rate increases, our muscles tense up, blood flows to our face, and we feel agitated and restless. This is known as the 'fight or flight' response, and is a physiological survival reaction which occurs in all mammals exposed to threatening situations, although it occurs in humans in response to both fear and anger. Essentially this means that the body is physically and psychologically preparing itself to either run or fight. This process involves the body drawing on its reserves of strength and agility to survive, and it does this via a mixture of chemical and physical transformations.

The central nervous system triggers a hormonal response in the brain for the body to take action. Adrenaline and excess cortisol are released into the bloodstream, which increases heart rate, contracts the blood vessels and dilates the air passages. Energy is released to the muscles by the reaction between oxygen and glucose (blood sugar), therefore blood sugar levels are elevated and our breathing rate increases to pump oxygen into the blood. Our pupils dilate so that we can see better and the brain averts its attention from non-emergency functions, so that blood flow can be diverted to the major muscle groups, hence digestion slows down, sex drive is depleted, and the capacity for rational or logical thought becomes impaired.

ACTIVITY 1.3

Consider the positive and protective aspects of anger. How and when can anger act as a force for good?

Anger also results in physical indicators such as the universal facial expressions we discussed earlier. Interestingly, all mammals express anger in a similar fashion: teeth are bared, eyes widen and stare, eyebrows are drawn together and down. Consider an angry dog protecting its puppies, and an angry home owner protecting their home. There's no mistaking the message both are sending: *go away and leave me alone!* These behavioural indicators of anger are designed for one purpose, to warn off a perceived threat.

However, threats can be interpreted in various ways depending on the life experience of the service user. While you may consider your social work role with a mother as that of an advocate, who is trying to intervene to help her to raise her children by offering support and guidance, she may have grown up hearing stories about social workers as 'home wreckers' who take away children and destroy families. Therefore your good intentions and professional responsibilities represent a potent threat to both she and her family, and she may very well respond to your attention with anger.

What we perceive as a threat can come in many forms, not just physical but psychological. Threats to someone's self-esteem, status or social role can be experienced every bit as powerfully as a physical threat. It is therefore very important to consider the manner in which your intervention as a social worker may threaten the service user. If we think about Jim and Mary from our case study, Jim has been employed for most of his adult life, and until recently been the main wage earner in the family. Jim's sense of self-esteem is likely to be tightly bound up with his sense of himself as a skilled worker and a good provider for his family. While the initial redundancy payment cushioned the blow of unemployment, the reality of job seeking and repeated rejections is invariably threatening Jim's status and self-esteem. Furthermore, his wife is now bringing in most of the money, and his son Tom is reaching the age where local factories want to employ him rather than Jim.

Jim's experience also illustrates another situation when angry feelings often arise, those occasions when our plans are thwarted, and we are frustrated in our intentions. Jim wants to work to earn money to support his family, yet his attempts to do so are unsuccessful. Failure to find work is affecting Jim's personality and impacting on the rest of his family.

CASE STUDY

Jim is becoming increasingly frustrated by his lack of employment. He finds it hard to get up in the morning when he has no job to go to; however, because he has slept late he is angry with himself for being lazy. When he does get up Mary is annoyed at him because she has had to get the children out to school and nursery alone, and feels that because Jim is now at home during the day, he should help out more. However, Mary also knows how irritable Jim has been lately and is scared to express her annoyance in case Jim loses his temper. Jim feels increasingly angry with Mary because she doesn't seem to understand how bad he is feeling. Usually a very close couple, Mary and Jim begin to grow apart.

The older children have noticed that Daddy seems cross all the time, and avoid spending time with him or making too much noise. However, Frank is too young to read the atmosphere in the home, and charges about being a normal, busy toddler. Frank is also

Continued

CASE STUDY *continued*

going through the 'terrible twos', and is occasionally difficult to manage, especially when he throws a tantrum. Previously a very 'hands-on' father, Jim now finds it very hard to be with Frank, and he has little patience for Frank's questions and childish chatter. Gradually Frank learns that Mummy is better to be with than Daddy and begins to avoid Jim.

On Wednesday Mary asked Jim to look after Frank while she went to work. Frank was running a slight temperature, and Mary was concerned he would become ill at nursery. When Mary left for work, Frank became very distressed, he began crying and shouting for his Mummy and pushing his Daddy away. Jim could feel himself getting very angry, but tried to control it and remained with Frank, trying to make him laugh and distract him from his tears. Frank continued to wail and push his Daddy away until Jim 'lost it'; he shook Frank and roared at Frank to 'shut up'. Frank stopped crying for a moment, stared at his Daddy, and then began crying even more than before.

Jim was shocked and ashamed that he had scared Frank; Jim also knew that he had been so angry he had nearly physically hurt his son. The experience frightened Jim and he was determined that it would never happen again. He decided that he would not allow himself to experience that level of anger for a second time. Although at first it was extremely difficult, Jim learnt how to bury and ignore the anger he was frequently experiencing.

A year and a half later, Jim was offered a job in a local factory; however, this was subject to an occupational health assessment. Jim welcomed this as an opportunity to ask his GP about the severe headaches, insomnia and nightmares he had been experiencing. When the GP checked Jim's blood pressure and cholesterol levels he found that both were dangerously elevated and that Jim was at high risk of developing serious heart problems. The GP was also concerned about Jim's mental health and has made a referral to the community mental health team.

COMMENT

As illustrated by Jim, frequent or chronic anger has the potential to cause harm on many levels. Not only can it destroy relationships and socially isolate the individual, it has been directly linked to family breakdown, anti-social behaviour by children, serious medical conditions and psychiatric difficulties. Because we instinctively know that anger can sometimes lead to uncontrolled and potentially damaging behaviours, our natural inclination is to avoid angry people. However, in social work we don't always have the luxury of this response, and so it is important to understand how anger affects both the individual experiencing the emotion, and those who are exposed to it. This is so that we can respond in a manner which doesn't increase the anger of the service user and which minimises the emotional impact on the social worker. Ways of managing anger and aggression will be looked at in detail in Chapter 3; for now we will explore the differences between anger and aggression.

What separates anger and aggression?

While anger is often associated with acts of aggression, the presence of one does not invariably result in the expression of the other. To put it very simply: anger is an emotion, aggression is an action. While anger is unquestionably a motivating force in many acts of aggression, it's certainly not always present. Experiencing anger does however increase the likelihood that someone will behave aggressively. This is due to the physiological changes associated with feeling angry, and their effect on our judgement and sense of restraint. If we consider Jim's verbally aggressive behaviour towards Frank we can see how Frank's challenging behaviour, and the additional stress of his son's rejection, coupled with Jim's ongoing frustration at his circumstances perhaps combined to push him over the edge, and behave in an uncharacteristically aggressive manner.

Phrases such as being 'pushed over the edge', or 'losing it', often refer to a perceived tipping point between anger and aggression. The fact that such phrases are common parlance illustrates how we understand aggression and anger existing on a continuum, which begins with irritation or annoyance and potentially ends with aggression. Anderson and Bushman (2002, p28) offer a useful definition of aggression:

> *Human aggression is any behaviour directed toward another individual that is carried out with the proximate (immediate) intent to cause harm. In addition, the perpetrator must believe that the behaviour will harm the target, and that the target is motivated to avoid the behaviour.*

Similarly, Geen (2001, p3) states that:

> *Aggression is the delivery of an aversive stimulus from one person to another, with intent to harm and with an expectation of causing such harm, when the other person is motivated to escape or avoid the stimulus.*

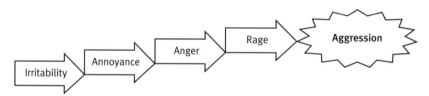

Figure 1.1 Stages leading to aggression

In the case of Jim and Frank, Jim's proximate intent was to stop Frank's behaviour by inflicting emotional and physical harm (shouting and shaking). Although Jim immediately regretted his actions and was filled with remorse, his behaviour was aggressive, and at the time it occurred, Jim (either unconsciously or consciously) believed that his son would stop what he was doing to avoid Jim's behaviour. However, this is where the complexity of defining aggression becomes apparent. Jim might argue that he was unaware of what he was doing to Frank, that he was blinded by rage and no longer in control of his behaviour. It is therefore not adequate or helpful to simply label behaviour as aggressive, we must endeavour to understand what kind of aggression is being demonstrated so that we can understand how to respond in an appropriate and safe way. We must also consider the ways in which aggression is demonstrated. The physical force associated with Jim's aggressive behaviour towards Frank is readily acknowledged as punitive aggression, but what about other less obvious acts of aggression such as destroying property, or spreading malicious gossip?

Studies of human aggression generally focus on two distinct types: affective aggression and instrumental aggression. The type of aggression illustrated by Jim is characterised as affective (or hostile, emotional, angry, reactive, impulsive) aggression. These terms generally refer to impulsive or thoughtless aggressive acts that arise from feelings of anger. The primary motivation underpinning affective aggression is the instinctual urge to harm the victim (who is usually the person or thing perceived to be provoking anger in the perpetrator). Rather than anger being the cause of affective aggression, it is viewed as an *intervening condition* (Geen, 2001, p4); this means that anger instigates and then guides the aggressive act towards the perceived provocation.

In contrast to affective aggression, instrumental (or cognitive, cold-blooded, premeditated) aggression refers to aggression whose primary objective is not to harm another person but to achieve another outcome which is important to the perpetrator. Harm may befall another individual as a result of this type of aggression but it is not the main goal of the behaviour. Take for example a person who is injured during a mugging. The incident is undeniably aggressive; however, the aggression was likely to have been purely instrumental (to facilitate the acquisition of someone's wallet), therefore its primary objective was unlikely to have been the injury to the victim. Similarly a soldier at war may undertake aggressive acts to serve his country, but the aggression is incidental to the desired outcome. Geen (2001, p4) defines instrumental aggression as *aggression which may or may not involve strong emotions but is motivated by concerns more important to the aggressor than the harm doing itself*. Accordingly, to define aggression as either instrumental or affective you must be able to identify the main factor motivating the behaviour. It is also important to note that on many occasions there may be a degree of overlap between these concepts, i.e. some acts of aggression may primarily be affective but also entail an instrumental element.

Identifying aggression

This may seem like a pointless area to explore. We have spent the last few pages talking about aggression; of course we know how to identify it! However, some acts of aggression are less obvious than verbal hostility or physical violence. When we consider aggression it's easy to assume it means manifestly hostile behaviour such as shouting, insulting or physically assaulting someone. However, we need to understand the subset of less evidently aggressive behaviours which also exist. Buss (1961) suggested a three-dimensional model which incorporated three categories of aggressive behaviour: physical-verbal, active-passive and direct-indirect, and within this model was able to identify eight types of aggressive acts. If we consider the model offered by Buss (1961, see Table 1.1), it becomes apparent that active or direct acts of aggression are relatively straightforward to identify, but passive or indirect aggression can be less obvious.

Table 1.1 Types of aggression

Type of aggression	Such as...
Physical-active-direct	Physically assaulting someone
Physical-active-indirect	Getting someone else to assault someone on your behalf. Damaging someone's property. Setting a bomb, etc.
Physical-passive-direct	Withholding a reference or obstructing someone doing what they want to do (sit-in protests)
Physical-passive-indirect	Refusing to perform necessary acts
Verbal-active-direct	Insulting someone or humiliating them in public
Verbal-active-indirect	Spreading gossip or malicious stories about someone
Verbal-passive-direct	Ignoring someone (giving them 'the cold shoulder', or 'the silent treatment')
Verbal-passive-indirect	Choosing not to defend someone falsely accused, or unfairly criticised

(Adapted from Buss, 1961)

Parrott and Giancola (2007) discuss an additional category of aggressive behaviour which we should also consider: postural aggression. This refers to non-verbal behaviour which does not involve physical contact between the aggressor and the target, such as threatening or intimidating facial expressions or body movements.

Passive and indirect aggression

As we can see from the examples above, the term 'indirect aggression' applies to situations where the victim or target is attacked indirectly, and the identity of the aggressor therefore remains concealed (such as when somebody spreads vicious gossip about another person). It's important to be aware that 'sneaky' activities such as poison pen letters, starting rumours or spreading nasty gossip are also aggressive acts, particularly in terms of the assumptions we make about gender and behaviour. Human males are generally considered more aggressive than females, and are certainly involved in more acts of physical violence, while females are considered the 'gentler sex', and less inclined to aggression. However, when indirect aggression is factored in, males and females are roughly equal. Psychologists, biologists and sociologists posit various theories as why this is so, which we will discuss further in the next chapter.

Like indirect aggression, passive aggression is another less evident act of aggression, and consequently trickier to identify. In contrast to active aggression, which entails an aggressor being actively involved in harming their target (such as damaging property), passive aggression is characterised by the intentional absence of activity with the primary intention to cause harm (such as refusing to speak out on someone's behalf).

It's worth mentioning that until relatively recently passive aggressive personality disorder (PAPD) was a defined diagnostic category in psychiatry, and you may still hear clients described in this way. Although no longer used as a clinical diagnosis, the term has endured as a descriptive label attached to individuals who consistently and repeatedly appear to actively comply with the needs and wishes of others, but in reality resist such demands via passive behaviour which masks underlying anger and aggression (Moore and Jefferson, 2004). While there is some common ground between PAPD, passive aggression and resistance, passive aggression as a personality type is characterised as a pattern of behaviour across all areas of a person's life, whereas resistance and passive aggression are specific behaviours undertaken in specific contexts.

Ambivalence

Ambivalence describes the emotional state of having co-existing positive and negative feelings about something or somebody. We acknowledge the existence of ambivalence when we talk about having mixed feelings about someone, or a love/hate relationship. In social work terms, ambivalence relates to the conflicting or contrasting emotions a client is likely to feel about different stages of intervention, and could be viewed as a set of scales. Consider the potential emotional response of a young mother who has been referred to family and child care social work because of concerns about her capacity to offer 'good enough' care to her children. During the initial stages of intervention the mother's ambivalence is very likely to be heavily weighted towards the negative side of the scales (see Figure 1.2), although there may be some co-existing positive emotions.

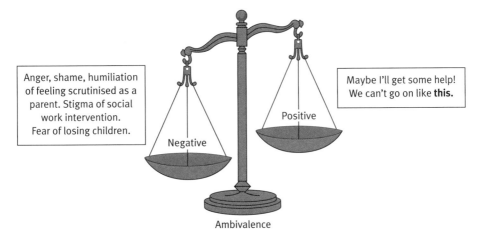

Anger, shame, humiliation of feeling scrutinised as a parent. Stigma of social work intervention. Fear of losing children.

Maybe I'll get some help! We can't go on like **this.**

Positive

Negative

Ambivalence

Figure 1.2 Conceptualising ambivalent feelings

Hopefully as intervention progresses, and a productive, respectful and honest relationship is established, the mother's ambivalence will move towards the other side of the scales, although a degree of ambivalence will probably always exist.

Resistance

The *Oxford English Dictionary* defines resistance simply as: *the act of resisting*. In social work the term generally applies to those clients who are unwilling, or feel coerced into engaging with you. This could be a mother who feels that she will lose her children if she doesn't attend weekly meetings at a family centre, or the school refuser who has been referred to a counsellor. Egan (2002, p171) refers to client resistance as the *shadow side* of helping, because clients don't talk openly about these feelings, and they are only apparent by analysing a client's behaviour and communication (or lack thereof).

Egan offers a frank description of resistant clients which gives a sense of the challenges associated with social work practice in this context:

Resistant clients, feeling abused, let everyone know that they have no need for help, show little willingness to establish a working relationship with helpers, and frequently try to con counsellors. They are often resentful, make active attempts to sabotage the helping process, or terminate the process prematurely. They can be testy or actually abusive or belligerent. Resistance ... is a matter of degree, and not all these behaviours in their most virulent forms are seen in all resistant clients.

(Egan, 2002, p165)

Although resistance could perceivably be confused with passive aggression, resistance differs in that although the client may choose to ignore your guidance or appear averse or reluctant to engage with you, this is not necessarily accompanied by an intention to cause harm. However, common sense would indicate that feelings of coercion, compulsion or duress are likely to lead to frustration and anger, and accordingly an increased likelihood of aggressive behaviours is associated with resistant clients.

An alternative definition of client resistance originates in Freudian psychoanalytic theory and subsequently, psychodynamic counselling. In psychodynamic terms, resistance usually refers to a client's inability, unwillingness or reluctance to deal with sensitive or particularly challenging issues, which accordingly prevents them from participating effectively in the therapeutic process. In this context, resistance is generally viewed as a client's conscious or unconscious attempts to protect themselves emotionally from interactions or events which challenge the coping mechanisms or defences they have created to manage how they feel about, or understand, their world.

In effect, this means that resistant clients may have very fixed ways of interpreting or understanding what's going on in their lives, or their role in what occurs to and around them. This in turn prevents clients from considering alternative approaches, perspectives or ways of behaving, and limits the effectiveness of any social work intervention which aims to facilitate change with the client.

There is risk associated with the use of resistance as a descriptive term for some clients, namely that it is a convenient way of depositing a social worker's failure to establish a rapport at the door of the client, which is both oppressive and unethical. Parton and O'Byrne (2000, p61) redefine resistance as *worker error*, whereby the social worker has failed to recognise resistance as the client's *unique way of cooperating* and therefore failed to offer their client a *constructive conversation*.

CHAPTER SUMMARY

Anger is a perfectly natural, if unpleasant, emotion experienced by all human beings; it is experienced on a continuum and can range in intensity from mild irritation or aggravation to fury or rage. Feeling angry is connected to autonomic (involuntary) physiological responses in our body to stimuli which are instinctively perceived to be threatening or negatively interfering with our life in some way. The body prepares itself physically and emotionally to fight or run.

Occasionally feeling angry in response to stress and the challenges of daily life is part of being human. It is an emotion we are entitled to, and which can positively enhance our own lives and others. However, frequent or chronic anger, suppressed anger and dysfunctional or aggressive behaviours arising from anger can be problematic.

Continued

Aggression is a universally acknowledged aspect of human behaviour, and the majority of us understand what is meant by the descriptive term 'aggressive'. However, defining aggression is more complicated. Studies of human aggression usually focus on affective aggression or instrumental aggression. The former usually occurs in response to anger or rage, whereas the latter refers to acts of aggression which are incidental to achieving another objective.

Given the context of practice and the critical issues impacting on clients, social workers are likely to encounter the emotions and behaviours discussed in this chapter on a regular basis, not only in the clients they work with, but also in their own emotional responses to the situations they encounter. There are multiple challenges associated with practice when clients feel angry, aggressive or resistant; not least that humanity's innate physiological response to these emotions is to drive their perceived source away. If you, your professional persona or the agency you represent happen to be this perceived source, then the barriers to engaging effectively are all too evident. Practice in these contexts will always be challenging; however, to aspire to the best outcomes, social workers need the capacity to protect themselves and others from the potential negative effects of these emotions, while also being able to anticipate, understand, manage and reflect on their own emotional responses and enable their clients to do the same.

FURTHER READING

Geen, RG (2001) *Human aggression*. 2nd edition. Buckingham: Open University Press.

This book offers a good introduction to psychological theories of aggression. It examines the mental and emotional processes which are thought to precede aggressive behaviours and analyses issues such as domestic violence and the social impact of violent media such as video games and movies. Geen also explores the relationship between gender, age, personality and aggression.

Howe, D (2008) *The emotionally intelligent social worker*. Basingstoke: Palgrave Macmillan.

This is a very accessible yet comprehensive introduction to the role of emotional intelligence. Howe discusses in depth how emotion can colour and distort how we understand ourselves and each other while emphasising the key role played by the therapeutic relationship between social worker and client.

Chapter 2

Understanding aggression and resistance

Aisling Monds-Watson

Introduction

This chapter will focus on biological, psychological and sociological theory relating to aggression and resistance. The chapter is divided into four sections.

- Theories of aggression related to human biology, instinct and evolution.

- Theories of aggression related to how humans respond to stimuli and experience.

- Theories of aggression related to how we think and learn.

- Theories of resistance.

Sometimes students (and social workers) have an ambivalent relationship with theoretical approaches, and believe that theory is pointless and convoluted, or that they should be concerned only with the reality or facts of clients' lives. However, facts need to be understood. By this I mean that knowing that something is the way it is is only half the story; we also need to understand why it might be the way it is. Failure to understand the 'why' of things severely limits our capacity to intervene effectively with clients. This is illustrated if we consider theory in relation to Jim's behaviour in the case study in the last chapter.

Jim has been waking up in the morning already feeling angry, and behaviours associated with this anger have been having a negative impact on Jim's marriage and family life; following an aggressive outburst with his two-year-old son, Jim has managed to suppress his anger but has also begun to experience headaches, nightmares and insomnia.

ACTIVITY **2.1**

Re-read the case study in Chapter 1 (page 3). What do you think is the cause of Jim's anger; where does it originate? Do you agree with the hypothesis that his anger is coming from his failure to find work?

COMMENT

The case study states that Jim's anger relates to his frustration at being unemployed; however, this assumption is in itself theoretical (the frustration-aggression hypothesis). Although it seems logical, and there is a body of evidence linking male unemployment with behavioural change and aggression, it may not be the only explanation. A biological perspective might point to Jim's subsequent diagnosis of dangerously high blood pressure and theorise that his emotions and behaviour were directly related to the physiological impact of this condition.

On the other hand, while unemployment may well be at the root of Jim's anger, it is likely to be more complicated than straightforward frustration. A psychodynamic perspective might suggest that the rejections Jim is experiencing in his efforts to find work are causing childhood memories of being excluded, unwanted or unloved to resurface and that this is intensifying Jim's emotional distress and contributing to his nightmares and insomnia. Repeated rejection might be reinforcing an already low self-esteem, and Jim may interpret this as evidence of his worthlessness. Alternatively, psychological theory may purport that possibly Jim always had difficulties dealing with anger, but this was sublimated within the catharsis offered by the heavy physical labour demanded in his place of work, an outlet no longer available to him.

Therefore in working with Jim, you would need to be conscious that while unemployment is a major factor in Jim's life, it may not be the sole cause of his emotional difficulties, and it would be simplistic to ascribe his behaviours and feelings to that singular fact. This is where good assessment skills and knowledge of theoretical frameworks relating to emotion and behaviour are vital to assist Jim in exploring, identifying and addressing the issues he is dealing with. Oko describes theory as *a set of related ideas and assumptions that are drawn upon to help explain a particular phenomenon ... they help us answer the question of what is going on, what can be done to help and why* (2011, p8).

Say for example, that assessment indicates Jim has always been quick to anger: the social worker might suggest that a cognitive behavioural approach could be employed to help Jim explore, understand and manage his emotions. Alternatively, referral to a counsellor may enable Jim to address traumatic issues from his childhood, improve his self-esteem, or perhaps productive employment is all Jim really needs to get back on track.

Theories of aggression and resistance: A word of warning

It is important to be able to structure our beliefs about why people behave in certain ways, within theoretical frameworks which help us to understand, explain and sometimes even anticipate how certain situations and experiences may be associated with certain behaviours and emotions. However, social workers must also consistently and consciously question the theories and assumptions they employ. This demands a capacity for reflection and critical thinking, and is where a balance has to be struck between the knowledge you bring to the job, your professional ethics and values, your statutory duties and the clients' own understandings of their lives.

There are a numerous theories and theoretical frameworks from a range of academic disciplines which attempt to either explain humanity's propensity for aggressive behaviour, or offer some contribution to understanding why aggression occurs, and they each offer valid explanations as to why people sometimes behave the way they do (see Table 2.1).

Although a few of these theories span two or more academic disciplines (such as socio-biological theory), each approach is in itself only partial, and while they will certainly offer insight into human behaviour, they will have shifting degrees of relevance and applicability to different situations. Therefore it is vital to consider their significance in relation to the multiplicity of factors likely to be involved in each practice setting, and the complexity of individual lives. The capacity to critically evaluate and consider the relevance and applicability of theory to your social work practice is an invariable, core component of anti-oppressive, ethical and effective interventions with clients.

Table 2.1 Theoretical frameworks which offer explanations for human behaviour

Psychological theories	Sociological theories	Biological/Evolutionary theories
Evolutionary theory	Interactionist/differential-association theory	Physiological/neurobiological theory
	Socio-biological theory	
	Psycho-social theory	Instinct theories
Psychodynamic theory		
Social learning theory	Relative deprivation theory	Frustration-aggression hypothesis

To make these theories easier to understand and also to partially illustrate how theory is interlinked and evolving, this chapter will consider and explore these various approaches by conceptualising them as three theoretical zones.

- Theories of aggression related to human biology, instinct and evolution.

- Theories of aggression related to how humans respond to stimuli and experience.

- Theories of aggression related to how we think and learn.

However, as you will see, there is a degree of overlap between these three zones, for example the frustration-aggression (F-A) hypothesis is a theory of aggression related to how humans respond to stimuli and experience. Yet the F-A hypothesis evolved in response to research, to encompass aspects of cognitive appraisal and attribution theory: theories related to how we think and learn. As you will see, theory is not set in stone; as scientific endeavour continues unabated, theories go in and out of fashion, or disappear altogether, depending on the evidence available.

Theories of aggression related to human biology, instinct and evolution

These theories consider aggression primarily from biological and evolutionary perspectives, but they also encompass psychodynamic theory in the form of Freud's work on instinct and drives. There has been a trend in recent years to dismiss Freudian approaches as irrelevant and even to denigrate psychoanalytic theory as oppressive, unethical and sexist; however, Freud's contribution to understanding human behaviour, particularly in terms of defence mechanisms and the influence of childhood experience, cannot be overestimated. While this chapter will confer upon Freud some of the recognition and criticism he deserves, it will begin with the basics: where human anger and aggression come from, and what they look like.

Physiological and neurobiological approaches to understanding anger and aggression

Indications of anger and aggression are usually expressed physically in our facial expressions, before they are acted on, so understanding the internal and external mani- festations of these emotional responses can help to anticipate and deal with them both as practitioners and individuals. Biological research can help us to understand the nature of anger and aggression from a physiological perspective, by offering insight into the role biochemical, genetic and hormonal make-up plays in how we experience, manage and convey emotions.

An extremely simplistic way to understand the structure of the human brain is to divide it into three parts: the brain stem, the limbic system and the cerebral cortex. In evolution- ary terms, the brain stem is the original part of the brain and is where all the automatic biological functions necessary for life reside. These are the psychological and physical operations that occur unconsciously (such as breathing, our blood pumping, our heart beating, and our muscles contracting). The next part of the brain to evolve was the limbic system; this surrounds the brain stem, controls our endocrine system and our automatic nervous system. Neurobiologists believe that the six basic emotions, including anger, originate in this very primitive area of the brain.

Then there is the cerebral cortex (the large part which looks a bit like a walnut), which makes up 80 per cent of the human brain, and can be divided (very roughly) into four parts, namely:

- the frontal lobe (which occupies from above our eyes to approximately the top of our heads);

- the temporal lobes (one on each side of the head above the ears);

- the parietal lobe (top of head to halfway down scalp);

- the occipital lobe (halfway down scalp to base of skull).

In relation to biological and physiological theories around emotion, particularly anger and aggression, the frontal and temporal lobes play a very important role because these areas of the brain are involved in the processing of information and the expression and regulation of emotion.

There can be no doubt that biochemical and neurological processes are sometimes directly linked to aggressive behaviours. Science has known for a long time that damage to certain areas of the brain is often accompanied by significant changes in personality. Sometimes this damage (particularly to the frontal lobes) results in dramatic and uncharacteris- tic behavioural changes and an escalation in aggressive urges and feelings of anger and frustration. Obviously this causes great distress to family and friends trying to come to terms with this 'new person' in their lives, who may look and sound the same, but who responds to the challenges of life in ways not previously known.

Neurological research in the field of neuromagnetic resonance imaging (neurological MRI scans) is also providing information about how the quality of early childhood relationships (first two years) affects the development of the brain, particularly those areas associated with emotion regulation and relationships.

Attachment theory (Bowlby, 1988) has long been used by social workers to understand the importance of a secure attachment relationship between a child and their primary care giver (see Crawford and Walker, 2010, pp50–55). However, recent neurological research is providing compelling and dramatic evidence of the role this bond plays in the developing brain. It is particularly important for social workers to understand and anticipate the difficulties around emotion regulation and relationship building that may be experienced by children (or adults) whose early attachment relationships have been less than adequate.

Biochemical theories of aggression

Chemicals, both those naturally occurring in the body and those imbibed via alcohol and drug use, also have a massive impact on our capacity to regulate our emotions. Research shows that males tend to be significantly more physically aggressive than females and that the male hormone testosterone is partially responsible for this. However, both very high and very low testosterone levels have been linked to aggression, as have low serotonin levels.

Alcohol and drug misuse are frequent factors in aggressive behaviour because of how they affect the prefrontal cortex (the very front of the frontal lobes). This part of the brain acts as a sort of filter, approving and disapproving certain behaviours and suppressing inappropriate impulses. When alcohol or certain drugs are introduced, this part of the brain can no longer effectively carry out its executive functions and this can lead to lack of inhibition, silly or dangerous behaviour, or aggression.

Physiological arousal level theories of aggression

Psychologists use the term 'physiological arousal level' to describe the types of consciousness associated with engagement in different activities. Although this sounds a bit complicated, it is really quite straightforward and simply refers to the behaviour of a person's autonomic nervous system. Consequently, a low arousal level equates to a relatively slow heart rate and reactivity level; for example, watching a boring film would equate to quite a low level of arousal, while taking your driving test or a going on a first date would probably represent a high level of arousal.

Although individual levels of arousal fluctuate depending on situation and circumstance, we each have an average arousal level which varies from low to high. In other words, some people are easily aroused, prone to anxiety or sensitive to stress and some are less so.

It would seem logical to assume from this that people who have a high level of arousal are more inclined to behave aggressively; however, research indicates the reverse: that actually those with very low arousal levels are more likely to behave in an anti-social or aggressive manner (Knyazev et al., 2002). This is thought to be because individuals with a low arousal level are more inclined to seek out thrill-inducing activity, which would cause physiological discomfort to someone with a high arousal level. Individuals with low arousal levels have been consistently found to be over-represented in studies of criminality and social deviance.

There is also evidence to suggest a strong genetic component to average arousal level. Research carried out with identical twins raised in different environments has demonstrated that irritability and impulsivity carry substantial heritability, in other words low levels of arousal often runs in families (Siever, 2008). However, you must be careful not to make assumptions about the behaviour of clients based on this knowledge. Labelling people according to their parental or familial characteristics is oppressive, judgemental and often inaccurate; it also ignores the capacity of human beings to moderate and manage their emotional states.

Instinct theories of aggression: Freud and Lorenz

Instinct theories assume aggression to be an unavoidable aspect of human existence which is inherent in our biological or psychological make-up. One of the first proponents of instinct theory was the famous psychologist Sigmund Freud, who asserted that humans were subject to two innate (inborn or instinctual) but opposing forces or drives, which he termed Eros and Thanatos. Eros was the drive towards life, survival, love and joy; while Thanatos was the death drive, the self-destructive part of us. To preserve life, Freud theorised that we directed the Thanatos or death drive outwards, i.e. we harm others to avoid harming ourselves.

Freud's theory of a death instinct contributed to what came to be known as a hydraulic model of aggression. This model assumes that aggression builds up (like steam in a pressure cooker), and has to be released via some form of cathartic activity (such as behaving aggressively towards someone else, watching violent sport, undertaking strenuous activity, or playing war games on the PC).

The catharsis provided by such activities was believed to release the pent-up negative energy associated with the instinct to aggress, leaving the person calm, relaxed and emotionally balanced once again. The notion of emotional purging via catharsis isn't unique to Freud; it can be traced back at least as far as Ancient Greece and Aristotle, who wrote of the capacity of theatre to calm and purify the emotions.

However popular and appealing notions about the beneficial effects of catharsis might be, this theory is also problematic. It is not possible to measure or observe Thanatos, nor does aggressive activity lessen the probability of future aggressive behaviour. Contrarily, the evidence indicates that in many instances aggression begets aggression.

Although derided by sophisticated, modern-day psychology and policy-orientated, evidence-based social work, it is not difficult to understand what Freud was endeavouring to explain. We all know of people who appear intent on self-destruction, and in practice you may occasionally encounter individuals who seem driven to destroy themselves and those around them. Having lived through the First World War, it is hardly surprising that Freud concluded that *the inclination to aggression is an original, self-subsisting instinctual disposition in man* (Freud, 1930, p313). Furthermore, there are occasional reports of individuals who apparently 'blow' for no obvious reason, and engage in uncharacteristically aggressive behaviour, such as the taxi driver Derek Bird's killing spree in Cumbria in 2010 (Carter et al., 2010).

Nor is Freud alone in asserting the notion that aggression is instinctual. Many scientists view aggression as a basic and primary survival instinct which humans share with the animal world. In 1966, Konrad Lorenz published a massively influential book entitled *On Aggression*, within which he argued that human aggression was a biological aspect of evolution designed to drive away predators, ensure reproduction and protect territory. Closely linked to Darwin's 'survival of the fittest', theory of evolution, Lorenz believed that an inherent instinct towards aggression was necessary for humans to evolve and adapt as rigorously and effectively as possible by 'weeding out' weakness. Lorenz also hypothesised that this allowed effective social structures to develop by establishing a social hierarchy based on strength. However, Lorenz's work was based on his careful observations of birds and reptiles; very few mammals and no higher primates (monkeys, apes, humans) were included; so while there is evidence to support an instinct theory of aggression in relation to birds and lizards, its applicability to humans is not as reliable.

Socio-biological theories of behaviour

Socio-biology focuses on the associations between genetic inheritance and human behaviour; in particular it presupposes connections between evolutionary theory and the differences in how males and females behave socially, including their propensity towards aggression. Although rooted in evolutionary Darwinian theory, socio-biological theory expands on evolutionary theory by arguing that physical characteristics are associated not only with survival of the fittest inherited via the evolutionary process, but also behavioural patterns. To understand the assertions of socio-biological theory it is vital to recap briefly and very basically on Darwinian theory.

- Genetic inheritance refers to the physical characteristics each species passes to its offspring via procreation.

- The physical characteristics associated with survival are those which fit most successfully with the environment within which that individual must exist.

- The process of natural selection ensures that those most successfully adapted to their environment are most likely to procreate (survival of the fittest).

- Via procreation the characteristics associated with survival are most likely to become encoded in the genetic make-up of the species.

However socio-biologists would argue that not only are physical characteristics associated with survival subject to evolution, but also behaviours. In other words, genetic factors influence behaviour to maximise the opportunity of the genetic code being passed on to the next generation. Socio-biological perspectives generally focus on differences between the behaviours of human males and females and (among other things) asserts that male aggression is genetically encoded to facilitate behaviour which will maximise his opportunity to transmit his genes to successive generations.

One of the strongest arguments against socio-biological and instinct theories of aggression is the contention that for aggression to be evolutionary or instinctual, it must also be universal. This assertion is refuted by the work of social anthropologists, such as Margaret Mead, who have studied the behaviour of different social groups, specifically remote and primitive tribes. In 1973, Erich Fromm reviewed the available anthropological research and concluded that out of the 30 tribes studied, only six could be described as aggressive and hostile. In fact evidence exists to show that our overriding instinct towards other human beings is potentially altruistic and protective. The vast majority of the tribes were societies in which *there is a minimum of hostility, violence or cruelty among people, no harsh treatment, hardly any crime, and the institution of war is absent or plays an exceedingly small role* (Fromm, 1973, p20).

Theories of aggression related to how humans respond to stimuli and experience

The frustration-aggression hypothesis

One of the earliest, most basic and perhaps most pragmatic psychological theories around aggression was put forward in 1939 by a small group of researchers at Yale University. John Dollard and his associates published a book which asserted that the bulk of human aggression could be explained by a few simple ideas, primarily that *the occurrence of aggressive behaviour always presupposes the existence of frustration and that the existence of frustration always leads to some form of aggression* (Dollard et al., 1939, p8).

The frustration-aggression (F-A) hypothesis was immensely influential, and had a massive impact on behavioural research in the late 1950s and 1960s. However, it fell out of favour due to subsequent research which demonstrated that this assertion was not reflective of the multiple factors associated with aggressive behaviour, particularly the influence of cognition on emotion and behaviour (i.e. the relationship between how we think, feel and act).

The frustration-aggression hypothesis was subsequently revised by Berkowitz (1989), who highlighted that all aggression doesn't necessarily arise from frustration, and queried whether frustration invariably resulted in aggression. Berkowitz produced a modified frustration-aggression hypothesis which acknowledged the validity of Dollard's common-sense recognition of the role frustration sometimes played in aggression, but also introduced two important and additional variables, primarily:

- the role of cognitive appraisal;

- the role of attribution.

In essence this means that to anticipate potentially aggressive encounters and understand why they occur, we have to pay attention to how people think, feel and make sense of what happens to them. Cognitive appraisal theory and attribution theory are fundamental components of cognitive theory, which is a psychological theory about how we think and learn, and we will return to them in the next part of this chapter.

RESEARCH SUMMARY

The two-factor theory of emotion (Schachter and Singer, 1962)

In 1962, Stanley Schachter and Jerome Singer undertook a social psychology experiment with 184 students to explore how we make sense of the physiological sensations experienced during emotional arousal. They divided the students into two groups and told them they were examining the effects of a new drug. However, the students were instead given an injection of either a stimulant (adrenaline) or a placebo (saline). Some of the students were told the truth (that they might experience a faster heart rate and rapid breathing), other students were told that they might experience a headache and numbness, and some were told nothing about the potential effects of the injection. The students were then individually asked to wait in a room with a member of the research team, whom the students believed to be another student taking part in the experiment. This person was instructed to behave in one of two ways, either as if they were frustrated and angry, or as if they were in an extremely playful, euphoric mood.

Schachter and Singer found that the students who had been told the truth about the injection attributed their physiological responses directly to the effects of the drug. However, the students who had been told that the drug would affect them differently or told nothing at all behaved in the same manner as the other person in the room; i.e. they became angry or excessively happy. The psychologists concluded that the students who knew about the effects of the drug were able to correctly attribute their physiological changes to the drug, whereas the students who were unable to do this believed their physiological responses were a reaction to the behaviour of the other person in the room.

The findings of this study formed the basis of 'cognitive labelling theory', and the 'two-factor theory of emotion'. This asserts that emotional experiences have two components: physiological arousal and cognition (the thinking process we use to make sense of and label how we feel). Basically this means that when we feel a certain way we look for environmental reasons to explain that emotion. Although subsequent research has revealed that the way we make sense of how we are feeling is much more complex than the factors in our immediate environment (i.e. we also look at many other relevant factors such as our understanding of ourselves and our own personal experience), Schachter and Singer's work was extremely influential in developing theories about how we understand and explain emotion, particularly in relation to cognitive appraisal theory.

Sociological theories of deviance

Deviance theory examines why a small percentage of people do not comply with what is commonly termed socially acceptable behaviour. Although socially unacceptable behaviour is not necessarily aggressive or destructive (for example, the bizarre behaviour of someone experiencing mental health difficulties), deviance theory offers particular insight into anti-social behaviour, and can help to understand and explain the context of social work practice in situations where there is potential for aggressive or hostile behaviour. Whereas psychological and biological theories of aggression tend to locate cause within the individual, sociological theories of aggression generally look to the social environment to explain aggression.

Numerous sociological theories exist in relation to deviant behaviour, but first you need to understand the sociological term 'social norms'. Basically social norms refer to the accepted and culturally sanctioned behaviours of a social group; whereas deviance is the violation of these social norms. However, social norms vary according to social grouping and location, so it is important to acknowledge that the concept of deviance depends on context. Particular behaviours are associated with different times of day/week, different cultural groups and different social settings; consider for example, the difference between physical aggression on a football pitch on a Saturday afternoon, a nightclub on a Saturday night and in a religious building on a Sunday morning.

Sociologists have come up with a number of theories about why deviance occurs, which we will explore briefly.

Control theory

Control theories of deviance originate in the work of Travis Hirschi (1969), who believed that whether an individual behaved in a deviant manner was dependent on the key variables:

- attachment;
- commitment;
- involvement;
- belief.

Fundamentally, a strong sense of attachment (strong social bonds) made it less likely that an individual would engage in deviance because of the commitment to social norms associated with attachment to their social group. Additionally, the level of practical involvement (or engagement) an individual had with their community, and how much they believed in the value system associated with that community, also decreased the likelihood of deviant behaviour.

Although control theory doesn't explain many aspects of anti-social behaviour, and has been criticised for being paternalistic and middle class, it does have some relevance when working with people who might feel disconnected or alienated from society, or who do not share your professional or personal value base.

ACTIVITY **2.2**

Consider a child who has experienced neglect and a lack of guidance at home, now placed in a residential facility, having lost any sense of community they had ever possessed. Are they likely to feel a sense of commitment or attachment to the staff? Will they share their values and accept the social norms within that facility? How will this affect the risk of socially unacceptable behaviours, given that other children in the facility are likely to be dealing with similar, disturbing experiences?

COMMENT

There is a balance in group care settings between considering the needs of the individual and those of every other individual, as well as bearing in mind group processes (see Chapter 8). It is important to consider how each individual will have their needs met within the group setting, but remember also that ideals often have to be tempered by the realities and constraints of resources and practice settings.

Relative deprivation theory

Relative deprivation theory (Merton, 1938) essentially describes how frustration arising from a sense of deprivation compared to others in your environment, can be linked to aggressive behaviour. Walter Runciman (1966) identified that for relative deprivation theory to be applicable, four conditions needed to be met (lack, knowledge, want, belief). Thus:

- the person must lack 'something';
- the person must know that other people have that 'something';
- the person must want that 'something';
- the person must believe that they can get that 'something'.

Although usually applied to groups of individuals who join up to revolt against perceived injustice, this theory can also be considered in terms of the frustration felt by a single client who feels that they are being deprived of something to which they are entitled.

Theories of aggression related to how we think and learn

Cognitive appraisal theory

Cognitive appraisal and attribution theory are key elements in anticipating and understanding how and why people behave the way they do, particularly in highly charged, emotional situations. An inability to 'tune in' to and understand how a client is appraising your intervention, and what attributes they are mentally assigning to you as a professional, will severely hamper your ability to effectively engage, respond sensitively and practise ethically and safely.

Cognitive appraisal theory evolved out of efforts to understand individual differences in affective responses to the same stimulus, or in layman's language: why different people respond in different ways to the same thing. In the simplest terms, appraisal theory basically describes how we appraise a situation according to the meanings we apportion to it, and the subsequent emotions and behaviours arising from those thoughts.

ACTIVITY **2.3**

- *Think about the meaning ascribed to a social worker's intervention by a mother whose child has been referred to family and child care services and who thinks that family and child care services are there to 'take children away' from 'bad' parents. How might she respond?*

- *Think about how a mother who had contact with social workers in her own childhood, and had a good experience of social work practice, might appraise the social worker's intervention. How might her response differ?*

COMMENT

The first mother is going to appraise the situation very differently from a mother who knows that she has been struggling to cope and thinks that she might now get the support she needs. Of course, how we appraise a situation is closely connected to our previous life experience. A mother who had contact with social workers in her own childhood, and had a good experience of social work practice, is going to have a very different appraisal from a mother who has been exposed to media scare stories and has had no direct previous involvement with social services.

Obviously the mother who appraises the intervention of social workers as a threat is more likely to respond defensively, become angry and potentially aggressive. This is why being clear about your role and responsibilities, communicating this in a sensitive but straightforward way, and revisiting it during the course of your involvement with clients is so important. You cannot assume that either you or the client is accurately appraising the situation unless you keep checking.

Cognitive attribution theory

Cognitive attribution theory is similar to appraisal theory in that it also acknowledges the cognitive dimension of how we feel and behave. However, attribution theory differs subtly, in that it focuses on how we feel and behave in relation to what we think about our own behaviour, and that of other people. Basically, attribution theory acknowledges that people have a fundamental need to explain why people do the things they do, and that we attribute meanings to our own and other people's behaviour.

Originating in the work of the social psychologist Heider (1958), attribution theory initially argued that: *the concepts people have about causality affects their social behaviour* (Lazaraus and Folkman, 1984, p271). In other words, why you think something happened affects how you feel about it, and how you behave in relation to it. A frequently quoted and simplistic example is that of the student who does well in an exam: if they attribute their success to hard work and intelligence, they are likely to feel they deserve the success and feel better about themselves than if they attribute their result to luck or an easy paper; subsequently they are more likely to work hard in the future.

A very important and relevant aspect of attribution theory (and comparable to Freud's theory of ego defence mechanisms, discussed below) is that generally people interpret what's going on in a way that allows them to maintain a positive self-image. Put simply, people attribute good things and bad things in ways that allow them to feel good about themselves.

In practice this means that a social worker telling a client something they don't want to hear might be dismissed as wrong, mean, deliberately misleading or malicious. Obviously this can then result in a less than effective working relationship, and potentially result in aggression and resistance from the client. Being aware of this aspect of attribution theory can help you to anticipate such situations and carefully plan how you deliver sensitive information, and address potentially skewed attributions.

Fundamental attribution errors

Another important aspect of attribution theory is that people tend to assume that others can act with agency. Essentially this means that we tend to ignore the external influences or restrictions on another person's behaviour and assume that they are independently choosing to behave in that manner. This is known as fundamental attribution error (or correspondence bias or the attribution effect) and was first highlighted by Lee Ross (1977).

We are all inclined to adopt fundamental attribution errors in regard to the unwelcome behaviours of others, and this has particular relevance when you, as a social worker, are acting as an agent of the state, for example when undertaking state-sanctioned and legislatively endorsed activity in child protection. Despite your professional role, you may be perceived by families as independently choosing to intrude on and disrupt their lives. Understanding this can sometimes help you to plan and deal emotionally with the challenges of practice.

It is also vital to consider your own attribution errors, particularly when working with challenging clients or difficult situations. An essential component of anti-oppressive practice and ethical social work is challenging the preconceptions, assumptions or attribution errors you may have about clients. Professionalism is about endeavouring to understand the variety and complexity of factors which may be influencing their behaviours, rather than misjudging and simply dismissing clients as bad, cruel, irresponsible or any number of other disparaging adjectives; failing to do so is oppressive, unhelpful, unprofessional and unethical.

Social learning theory

Psychological theories of aggression related to how we learn from our social environment assert that individuals learn to behave aggressively by observing this behaviour in others and also by perceiving this to have positive rewards. The relevance of social learning theories of aggression is reinforced by evidence that cultures and subcultures which condone aggressive behaviour are known to be significantly more violent than those who don't (Fromm, 1973). Basically when aggression is promoted culturally (via the media, education system, peer group, etc.) it is more likely to occur, whereas within cultures which discourage aggression, violence is less likely.

The main exponents of social learning theories of aggression were Albert Bandura and Walters (1963), who designed the famous Bobo doll experiment to study three aspects of aggression.

- How patterns of aggressive behaviour develop.

- What provokes aggression?

- What sustains or causes reoccurrence of aggression?

They first exposed children to a video of an adult viciously attacking a Bobo doll (an inflatable, child-sized, plastic doll, which was weighted at the base to make it stand up). The adult hit the doll with a mallet, punched it, threw it to the floor, sat on it, threw balls at it, and generally gave the doll a 'good seeing to' (Bandura et al. called this modelling). After witnessing this, the children were left in a room full of attractive toys which they weren't allowed to play with, thereby frustrating the children (Bandura et al. called this retention because the frustrated children retained the memory of the aggressive behaviour). Finally the children were individually allowed to play with both the Bobo doll and the toys the adults had used to attack it.

The researchers found that 88 per cent of the 66 children (half male, half female) who took part in the experiment repeated the aggressive behaviour they had seen on the video. When followed up eight months later, 40 per cent of the children still responded to the Bobo doll in an aggressive way. A particularly interesting part of the Bobo doll research was the experiment undertaken to explore the role of gender. The researchers divided another group of children into groups of 12 (6 female and 6 male) to see how gender affected how the children modelled the adult behaviour.

- Group 1 watched an adult male acting aggressively.

- Group 2 watched an adult female acting aggressively.

- Group 3 watched an adult male acting non-aggressively.

- Group 4 watched an adult female acting non-aggressively.

The researchers found that overall the boys were almost twice as likely as the girls to copy the aggressive behaviour they had witnessed. The boys were also twice as likely to copy the aggressive behaviour of an adult male than a female; while the girls were nearly twice as likely to copy a female role model. When the children had watched either male or female adults playing non-aggressively with the Bobo doll, the children subsequently demonstrated little aggressive behaviour when they were finally allowed to play with the doll. The experiment led to Bandura et al. formulating their theory of observational learning, because the children learnt their behaviours by observing the adults.

Bandura and his colleagues also carried out a version of the Bobo doll experiment where the aggressive adults were either punished or rewarded for their behaviour. The researchers found that although the children learnt the aggressive behaviour, whether or not they 'performed' it was based on whether they had seen the aggression rewarded or punished. Bandura called this vicarious conditioning, which simply means that people can be conditioned to behave in certain ways by watching what happens to others.

Bandura et al.'s 1961 Bobo doll experiment endures as possibly the most influential and famous piece of research in relation to aggression theory. Fundamentally, social learning theory asserts that human aggression is: *a learned conduct that, like other forms of social behaviour, is under stimulus, reinforcement, and cognitive control* (Bandura, 1980, p146).

Interestingly, social learning theorists allow for the presence of the frustration-aggression hypothesis, and recognise that frustration is likely to be a potential instigator of aggression. However, they assert that aggressive behaviours must first be learnt, rather than pre-existing as an instinctual response to frustration or other negative stimuli.

ACTIVITY 2.4

Read the following quote from Daniel Goleman and think about what you have just read about social learning theory:

> *Family life is our first school for emotional learning; in this intimate cauldron we learn how to feel about ourselves and how others will react to our feelings; how to think about these feelings and what choices we have in reacting; how to read and express hopes and fears. This emotional schooling operates not just through the things that parents say and do directly to children, but also in the models they offer for handling their own feelings and those that pass between husband and wife ... How parents treat their children – whether with harsh discipline or empathic understanding, with indifference or warmth and so on – has deep and lasting consequences for the child's emotional life.*

> (Goleman, 1995, p189)

Think about the case study in the previous chapter. How might Jim's behaviour in the home affect the social learning of his children?

What other factors might influence their behaviours?

COMMENT

There is research that indicates that authoritative parenting – neither harshly authoritarian nor flabbily permissive – is the best environment for children to develop the skills needed to live a fulfilling adult life with a health interdependence within society (neither overdependent nor becoming isolated through excessive independence). The influence of parenting style on the development of children should not be underestimated.

Interactionist or differential-association theory

Differential-association theory is a sociological theory about how humans develop behaviours in relation to how they interact with their environment. Proposed by Edwin Sutherland (in 1924), it has been very influential in the study of criminology and deviance. Essentially another theory related to how we think and learn, differential-association theory shares much with social learning theory, and is premised on the assertion that if someone grows up in an environment where criminal activity or aggression are valued and promoted, then the child will learn a set of values and behaviours to support such activity.

There is evidence to suggest that anti-social behaviour can run in families. When Osborne and West (1982) compared criminality among sons of fathers with criminal convictions against those without, they found that 40 per cent of the convicts' sons had been convicted of a crime by the age of 18, as opposed to only 13 per cent of sons of non-criminal fathers. However, such research could also be argued as supporting evidence for genetic inheritance, and as such should be taken with a degree of scepticism. The fact that 60 per cent of those with criminal fathers didn't have a conviction is also worth considering in relation to the characteristics sometimes attributed to the children of criminals.

RESEARCH SUMMARY

Do violent games make children aggressive?

Since the inception of the relatively innocent arcade video game, and its subsequent evolution to the highly complex, super-real gaming consoles now found in most teenage bedrooms, researchers from various academic disciplines have been actively engaged in trying to establish whether or not playing these games results in increased levels of aggression and violence. Repeatedly, the evidence seems to indicate that, yes, it does. Not only does exposure to violent television and participation in aggressive games appear to increase an individual's propensity to behave aggressively, it also makes them increasingly insensitive to the impact of violence.

However, research by Feshbach and Singer in 1971 offers an alternative perspective. They recorded the aggressive behaviours exhibited by a group of teenage boys for six weeks, half of whom regularly watched television containing aggressive or violent content, and half who did not. Rather than finding increased incidents of aggression within the group exposed to violent television, the researchers actually found the opposite. The boys who didn't watch aggressive television were demonstrably more aggressive than those who did. Feshbach and Singer believed this was because the boys were offered a form of catharsis via their identification with the aggressive characters on the television which made them less inclined to behave aggressively in the real world.

In 2010 Anderson and colleagues undertook analysis of all the available research relating to violence and game playing worldwide. They concluded that there was strong evidence to suggest that exposure to violent video game play was associated with a small increase in aggressive thinking and behaviour, and slightly decreased levels of empathy and pro-social behaviour, regardless of gender, culture or ethnicity. However, others (Ferguson and Kilburn, 2010; Freedman, 2002) dispute this finding, pointing out that proportionally, recorded incidences of youth aggression have actually decreased in recent years, even with increased exposure to violent media.

So, despite the thousands of research studies about the effects of game playing and television on aggression, the jury is still out. However, one thing the researchers all agree on is that exposure to violent media is unlikely to be the sole cause of aggressive

Continued

behaviour. While there does appear to be a small correlation between children's exposure to media violence and subsequent aggressive/anti-social behaviour (Ferguson and Kilburn, 2010), this is relatively minor in terms of the other influences on a child's life and has to be considered in the context of their home environment, biological and genetic factors, and social relationships.

Psychodynamic theories related to working with resistant clients

Some of the most helpful and insightful theories in relation to understanding client resistance are found in psychodynamic theory where they evolved from the efforts of psychotherapists to understand why:

> some painfully distressed patients seeking assistance from expensive and highly trained professionals reject their therapists' best advice, fail to act in their own best interests, and do not respond to the most effective interventions that can be mustered on their behalf.

> (Beutler et al., 2002, p207).

This observation is likely to be depressingly familiar to experienced social workers. Resistant clients can be a massive source of frustration, demoralisation and worry as well as a contributory factor to burn-out among practitioners.

In the last chapter we mentioned clients who seem to be 'stuck on self-destruct', or who appear to actively resist all attempts to enhance or improve their lives. A theoretical understanding of why some people behave this way can help you to pre-empt, comprehend and accommodate their resistance, while allowing you to plan, phase and manage how you can best engage and intervene in their lives. Most importantly, having a sound theoretical concept of resistance can sustain you to carry on working patiently and effectively with some very challenging clients.

Defence mechanisms

One of the earliest and most enduring attempts to gain a basic understanding of psychological resistance is rooted in Freud's *The ego and the mechanisms of defense* (1937), within which Freud delineated the existence and role of hypothetical defence mechanisms. Much has been written about defence mechanisms and Freud's original idea has been adapted, expanded, refuted, critiqued and researched for many years. Research has evidenced their existence and the identification, analysis and management of psychological defence mechanisms are now key aspects of modern clinical psychology and psychiatric practice (Cramer, 2006). However, to develop even the most fundamental grasp of how humans employ defence mechanisms, we must first develop an extremely basic understanding of Freud's psychodynamic theories of the mind. The two aspects to this are:

- Freud's theory of consciousness;

- Freud's theory of the structure of the mind or psyche.

Freud believed that the human mind or psyche was composed of three parts. These are:

- the id, which is the want-driven, childish part of our personality which demands immediate gratification of all desires;

- the superego, which is our internalised learning from our parents and society about what is good and bad, right and wrong;

- the ego, which acts as a mediator between the id and superego.

Essentially Freud saw the ego as the part of the human mind which experiences and responds to both the real world and our internal wants and desires. To allow us to live in a way that is compatible with what our friends, our family and society deem to be acceptable, the ego moderates between the demands of the id and the stern morality of the superego to find a compromise between what we want and how we go about getting it. Freud called this the modification of the pleasure principle in relation to the reality principle.

However, Freud also believed that these three aspects of our personality were active in different parts of our consciousness. The conscious is the small part of our mind which we have ready access to, then there is the pre-conscious part of our mind, which we have partial access to, but have to think about and bring to our conscious mind via the act of remembering or thinking. The ego operates in both our conscious and pre-conscious. Freud believed that most of our mind was subconscious or unconscious: this is where unpleasant, unacceptable and disturbing memories, experiences and thoughts are buried; and this is where the id resides. Freud believed that although we can't access our unconscious, it still has immense influence over how we think, feel and behave. Because the superego evolves from our learning and experience in both the past and present (about what is socially acceptable or morally good), it operates on all three levels of consciousness.

In relation to defence mechanisms, Freud asserted that when there is a conflict between the id and the superego which cannot be moderated via a compromise by the ego, then anxiety or psychological discomfort occurs. The ego manages this anxiety by blocking the impulses of the id, and either redirecting them to a socially acceptable outlet or burying them in the unconscious. Consider the very simplistic example of the woman who is so angered and hurt by her husband's infidelity that she lovingly provides him with a diet of high-calorie, high-cholesterol, heart-attack-inducing meals accompanied by wines and beautiful desserts. The notion that she unconsciously wants to harm him doesn't even enter her head, nor does the fact that he has a long-standing history of heart disease (although she sometimes dreams about his funeral!). This type of defence is known as reaction formation. Instead of demonstrating her anger and hurt she transforms it into a socially and personally acceptable (but equally damaging) activity.

Modern psychological theory has expanded Freud's concept of ego defence mechanisms to also encompass threats to self-esteem, self-identity and to how we view our world. So in essence, defence mechanisms are now understood as unconscious psychological systems of protection against anything that seriously threatens our sense of who we are, who we think we are, where we are or who we want to be. Obviously some of us are more secure in our sense of these things than others. Someone who missed out on a secure loving childhood is less likely to feel secure in their sense of self-worth than someone who has not. However, instead of seeking out the love and affection that they have missed out on, their defence might be to never let anyone get emotionally close, and in this way they avoid the pain of rejection and can deny that they ever needed anyone, anyway. Interestingly, this corresponds to the insecure avoidant attachment pattern, which Mary Ainsworth et al. (1978) theorised might arise in an infant as a result of inconsistent or unreliable care from their primary care giver.

People employ numerous defence mechanisms; some are considered to be adaptive and mature such as art, humour, sport, and some are considered to be damaging, immature or even pathological. Social workers are likely to encounter the majority of defence mechanisms during their career – hardly surprising given that their work frequently involves delivering difficult truths and helping people to manage painful and challenging emotions. Detailed discussion of the variety of ways in which some clients may unconsciously resist these processes is not feasible within the scope of this book, but some of the more common, damaging defence mechanisms are listed below.

- Repression, when an experience or knowledge which is too painful or disturbing to deal with is simply repressed or forgotten.

- Denial, protecting oneself from psychological pain or trauma by simply denying the reality of a situation or experience.

- Rationalisation, creating an excuse for doing something unacceptable rather than acknowledging the emotional impact or reality of what has happened.

- Projection, projecting the cause of unacceptable actions onto others; for example a paedophile who asserts that a child seduced them by dressing provocatively.

- Displacement, moving feelings (usually fear, anger or anxiety) about one part of your life to something not as threatening; for example the bullied employee going home and shouting at their children.

- Emotional insulation and detachment, disengaging emotionally from the world around you so that you can no longer be hurt or disappointed.

- Regression, dealing with psychological challenges by regressing to an earlier (possibly infantile) stage.

- Acting out, dealing with challenging emotions such as anxiety, anger, fear or frustration by inappropriately expressing them in violent, anti-social or unacceptable behaviour.

However, we all use defence mechanisms to some degree at some time, and describing a client as resistant can be a useful defence mechanism for a social worker who is finding their work with a client ineffective. Understanding the type of defence mechanism you think is being employed can offer some insight into why a client is reluctant or resistant. However, you also need to consider if it is the intervention itself that is driving the client away.

Beutler et al. (2002) highlight that contemporary theories of resistance are based on a number of generalisable assumptions, primarily that:

- everyone values freedom of choice and action;

- everyone reacts negatively to real or perceived challenges to their freedom.

Psychodynamic theory has developed the term 'reactance arousal' to describe client resistance which arises from a perceived loss of interpersonal freedom within the therapeutic relationship. To counter reactance arousal Beutler et al. suggest the following approach, which sounds suspiciously like old-fashioned, ethical, partnership-based social work practice.

- Acknowledge and reflect the client's concerns.

- Discuss the therapeutic relationship.

- Negotiate an agreeable and acceptable contract regarding the intervention.

(Beutler et al., 2002, p215)

CHAPTER SUMMARY

This chapter has offered an overview of some of the theories which may be relevant to practice in situations where there is anger, aggression or resistance. However, while these theories offer some explanation of challenging emotional states, and can help to inform the approach we take as social workers, they are not necessarily evidence-based and they cannot be relied on to fully explain all situations of anger, aggression or resistance that you may encounter.

Each of these theoretical approaches is in its own way reductionist, i.e. it doesn't fully acknowledge the intricacy and multidimensionality of human existence, and the composite and complex social, psychological and biological aspects of people's lives. While each theory contributes to our understanding, they have different levels of relevance to different situations and must therefore be critically evaluated in the context of the client's specific circumstances.

FURTHER READING

Campbell, A (1993) *Men, women and aggression*. New York: Basic Books.

This is a fascinating book which explores aggressive behaviour from a gender perspective and examines popular assumptions about why men and women behave differently.

Ingleby, E (2010) *Applied psychology for social work*. 2nd edition. Exeter: Learning Matters.

This provides an excellent overview of the relevance and applicability of psychological theory to practice. The author offers numerous practice examples and critically evaluates the therapeutic value of various psychological approaches.

Chapter 3

Avoiding assault and defusing aggression

Brian J Taylor

Introduction

This chapter focuses on general principles and pointers for avoiding assault and defusing aggression. It gives ideas to consider in managing a safer environment and developing skills in defusing an aggressive situation. We focus on approaches that you might take in any setting to avoid being the victim of assault and to defuse escalating volatile situations. The intention of this chapter is to locate the discussion in later chapters by focusing here on the more extreme situations of aggression, and the legal and practical issues involved with these. The chapters that follow consider aspects that are relevant to understanding a particular client group and creating a care context that will make violence less likely and social work intervention more productive. By attending to these personal safety issues you will be more confident and helpful in your social work role, less likely to be assaulted, and more able to engage resistant clients.

It is beyond the scope of this book to attempt to teach the physical aspects of personal safety such as breakaway techniques to escape from being held by an aggressor or team restraint methods. These are an important part of your knowledge and skills as appropriate to your role, and complement the material in this book. Such physical skills cannot be learnt from a textbook and must be practised so as to develop muscle memory, not just head knowledge. You should seek training from your employer on this. It is your responsibility as an individual employee and professional to undertake personal safety training, to use equipment provided, to work within policies and procedures and to exercise judgement about the best course of action in any particular situation. It is beyond the scope of this book to consider the responsibilities of employers to provide training, equipment, policies and procedures in relation to reducing the risk of injury to their staff, including through assault (Health and Safety at Work Act 1974 Section 2; Health and Safety at Work (NI) Order, 1978, both as subsequently amended). Your professional organisation – such as the British Association of Social Workers – can advise you of your legal rights regarding such issues.

> *This chapter gives you some ideas to help you to reflect on your practice and instinctive reactions to challenging situations. In any particular situation only you can decide what action to take to try to avoid assault, defuse aggression or seek to engage a reluctant client or family. Not all ideas will work for all people in every situation. Despite all the precautions we might take, on some occasions some professionals are injured by clients. These ideas are to prompt your thinking about how to respond to difficult situations so as to reduce the likelihood and seriousness of assault and achieve the best possible outcome in the circumstances for the client, family, other professionals, others in society and yourself.*

> *Any reference to legal matters is intended only as an introductory guide for general education by a non-lawyer for non-lawyers. Do not rely upon this book as a substitute for legal advice on any individual set of circumstances. In relation to legal matters, this chapter aims to inform you about general principles and issues so that you are more able to identify when legal advice needs to be sought, and enable you to better understand and discuss the issues. This book does not purport to address the detailed legal requirements in any particular jurisdiction, but to educate on general principles that are common in democratic countries.*

Awareness of danger of assault

In our social work practice most of our attention is on the needs of our clients and the risks they face (Taylor, 2006). Sometimes we are concerned about the threat posed by a client to others, such as a family member, other occupants of the living accommodation or the wider society. However, you should also consider the possible danger to yourself in each client contact. Any risk assessment or risk management activity should consider the risks posed to you, other social care workers and other professionals as well as the risks to the client, family and others in society. Your ability to recognise a person or situation as being potentially dangerous makes you safer. If you are aware of danger you are able to plan and take steps, even if it is only small steps that are required, to make yourself safer. Such awareness involves knowing what to be aware of, and disciplining yourself to pay attention. The ultimate success of your development of knowledge and skills is when nothing happens! Hence positive feedback on your efforts to stay safe will be very limited and you need to remain disciplined and focused to continue to plan your working life with sufficient attention to personal safety.

It is important that if you are the victim of assault you do not blame yourself. The perpetrator is responsible for his or her actions. At the same time as social workers we are electing to work with vulnerable people often at a point of crisis and distress. It is inevitable that aggressive behaviour will sometimes occur given fallen human nature. Sometimes the perceptions of clients and of helpers can be markedly different about the care environment or the circumstances of the interview or other intervention. What might not seem stressful to a professional social worker may be so to a particular client in certain circumstances.

RESEARCH SUMMARY

Eighty patients and 82 nurses from three inpatient mental health wards were surveyed using the Management of Aggression and Violence Attitude Scale. A further five patients and five nurses from the same sample participated in a number of follow-up interviews. Patients perceived environmental conditions and poor communication to be a significant precursor of aggressive behaviour. Nurses, in comparison, viewed the patients' mental illnesses to be the main reason for aggression, although the negative impact of the inpatient environment was recognised. From interview responses it was evident that both sets of respondents were dissatisfied with the restrictive and under-resourced provision that tended to increase interpersonal tensions. Training in fundamental therapeutic communication skills was advocated by patients, while the need for greater attention to organisational deficits was advocated by nurses.

(Duxbury and Whittington, 2004)

COMMENT

The earlier that you detect and recognise a potential problem situation, the more options you have to resolve it. You need to aim to develop a good mental map of relevant factors such as those suggested below. Paying attention involves adjusting your conscious focus to include what is relevant to personal safety in every situation. The only effective personal safety strategies are those that you build in to your day-to-day behaviour so that they become unconscious habits through repetition. The key is to anticipate and recognise danger and to take action to avoid it. There are a number of features that should heighten your awareness of possible assault and help to keep you safe. We will consider these under the headings of: the task, the client, other people, the environment and your own reactions.

Awareness – the task

Before visiting or carrying out a visit to a client's home, consider the task that you are undertaking from the perspective of the client and others. Are you charged with conveying bad news? Are you involved in compulsory safeguarding intervention such as possibly removing children from their parents (Ferguson, 2005)? Are you involved in considering such compulsory interventions and the build-up to action possibly being taken? Is the situation one of matrimonial dispute or domestic violence where you might become an unwitting third party on whom anger is vented? Are you involved in exercising parental authority such as in a children's home?

Awareness – the client

It is important that you try to find out something about a client before visiting in their own home. If this is a person with a history of violent offences or abuse, then exercise caution about the arrangements that you make. You should seek to understand the context of the vulnerabilities and trigger factors for possible aggressiveness by this type of client (Taylor, 2010). Be aware of appearance as a clue to possible assault. Not everyone dressed in black leather and chains is aggressive but appearance may give a clue to potential aggression. A person who presents as more unkempt than usual may be going through a rough patch and may not be as amenable to work with as usual. People have different expectations of personal space, but someone who invades your personal space may be more aggressive. An aggressive person may make excessive eye contact or avoid eye contact, and may start to take up more confrontational body positions and postures. Be alert to a person who seems anxious: fiddling, changing position, frowning, biting lips, etc. Be aware of signs of frustration: head-shaking, sighing and such like. Be alert to cues to aggression such as wagging or jabbing a finger, tense posture, flexing arms or clenched fists. Listen for tone of voice, particularly if it changes to become menacing.

Awareness – the family and environment

If you are visiting a client at their own home, remember to consider who else might be in the home. What family members, friends or others might be there? Are there neighbours who might have an interest in your visit for less than desirable reasons? What do you know of the neighbourhood and the safety of the route that you intend to travel? If you start to become concerned when inside a home, look around quietly for objects that might be used as weapons. Look for possible escape routes and begin to readjust your position if this can be done without arousing suspicion. Consider how you can summon assistance.

Awareness – your own reaction

It is very important that you remain aware of your own bodily and emotional reactions relating to fear, stress and tension. Do not just ignore such feelings. Your feelings are a prompt to you to consider what action to take. This might be a conscious effort to control your feelings and convey calmness through your own behaviours. However, it may reach a stage where your feelings are a prompt to make a quick exit, perhaps with a suitable excuse.

It may be that particular situations 'press a button' for you because of previous life experience. We all have aggressive impulses, and there may be some interaction between the particular way this client is behaving and your own internal ways of managing aggressive feelings. Some of us have suffered abuse and violence at home or in the street. Certain situations may be particularly stressful if related to personal circumstances. Through reflection in whatever form – often with a spiritual component – we work through our life experiences and instinctive feelings to grow in maturity and in our capacity to use our life experience to help others. If you discover that you have unresolved issues or harmful aggressive impulses, you should seek help from a suitable counsellor.

Avoiding harm

This section gives some pointers for reflection on your practice and daily habits that may assist you in reassessing your behaviours and responses so as to be less likely to be assaulted, and to reduce the seriousness of any assault that occurs. In any situation only you can decide what action you are going to take. These ideas are for consideration to prompt you to reflect on your routines, plans and possible action you might take.

Personal safety in the office and office interviews

The office can seem a safe place until you have experience of a violent client there. If there is any possibility of violence, take a moment to think of your personal safety. If you feel uneasy, take appropriate protective steps. There should be a system so that you can summon assistance through a panic button or calling someone on site if necessary.

- Is a joint interview required?
- Is there any dangerous object in the interview room that might be used as a weapon?
- How will you position yourself so as to be able to exit quickly if necessary?
- Is the seating arrangement conducive to being non-confrontational?

Personal safety travelling by car

Field social workers typically travel by car to see their clients, and visit clients in their own home more often than most professionals. It is important to keep your car serviced and have a working torch and camera with you. In inclement weather take precautions such as warm clothing, food and drink. In planning your route, remember that roads where other cars are travelling may be safer if you were to break down. If you are in difficulty and a stranger offers to help, ask the person to get help rather than getting out of your car. To help a stranded motorist, make a telephone call for them. If you think you are being followed: stay in the car; ensure that it is locked; flash the lights and sound the horn for attention. Have your keys in your hand as you approach your car so that you do not spend time fumbling at the car door trying to find them. Look inside before entering your car to ensure no one is hiding in it. Lock your car when entering as well as when leaving it.

- When you park, will it will be safe to return to this spot later?
- Can you park so as to be able to drive away quickly, particularly if there are dangers in this house or estate?
- Could someone 'tailgate', i.e. get into a building or car park by following close behind you and taking advantage of your entry permission (swipe card or key, etc.)?

Personal safety travelling by taxi or public transport

Sometimes you may travel by public transport or taxi. Pre-book a licensed taxi for greater safety. If you are uneasy about the taxicab or driver, don't get in.

- Choose a seat on a bus within sight or earshot of the driver.
- Choose a carriage in a train where there are other people.
- If you feel uneasy, change seats.
- If you become uneasy in a taxi, ask to get out where there are people, in a well-lit area.

Personal safety in the street

Even though you will probably travel in a vehicle, part of your journeys will be on foot. Keep alert to people and places and think ahead. Be aware of your surroundings and possible dangers. Plan your journey and avoid short-cuts through unlit or deserted areas. Walk with purpose and confidence.

If possible walk with or near someone. Avoid showing that you are carrying money or valuable items. Be discreet with your purse, wallet or handbag.

- Walk near to the kerb and away from building entrances and alleyways.
- Maintain confident normal eye contact with people you pass; avoid looking anxious.
- If you suspect that you are being followed, cross the road and go to the nearest house, petrol station or open business premises and call the police.
- Do not give your name, address or place of employment to strangers.
- Shout for help if you are feeling threatened.
- If someone tries to take something from you in the street it might be better just to let them take it rather than to get into a confrontation and risk injury.

Personal safety in a client's home

Many assaults on social workers occur in the client's home. Find out about the person and situation prior to the visit. Check who else might be present and whether this poses a threat. If a joint interview is required, ask for this. Does someone know where you are going and when you expect to return? Before you go on a home visit ensure that someone will make enquiries if you do not turn up by a certain time. Dress appropriately, avoiding cultural or sexual provocation. Wear footwear in which you can run if necessary. Avoid wearing a tie, necklace, earrings or long, loose hair that might be pulled.

- Position yourself to exit the house quickly and escape if necessary.

- Select a non-confrontational seating arrangement.

- Be wary of situations (e.g. kitchens) where available objects might be used as weapons.

Defusing escalating aggression

Sadly aggression is so common in social work practice that reducing aggression has become a part of the social work knowledge and skills curriculum. Beyond a common knowledge base the skills in defusing escalating aggression are subtle and personal and hence difficult to describe and teach. One can admire a professional handling a difficult situation well; it is harder to describe what made the response effective and worth emulating. The key issue is that if you start to get uneasy about escalating emotions then you need to focus on calming the situation and attending to your own safety.

Emotional coping

A core skill in coping with aggression is to know yourself. If you know how you might react under provocation it can help you in dealing with situations. A strong sense of your own self-worth and values, the ability to reflect on your own feelings and the generosity to help others despite their behaviour towards you, all help in coping with aggressiveness.

Moral authority

One aspect of reducing escalating aggression might be described as moral authority. As a social worker, like other professionals, the context of violence at work is normally different from when you are a member of the general public on the street. There is some sort of relationship between you and the client. That relationship might become strained due to the task that you have to undertake or some misunderstanding or unrealistic expectations or needs. However, violence at work is unlikely to be the kind of irrational violence for its own sake that might be encountered on the street late on a Saturday night. Sometimes referring back to the basis of your helping relationship with the client can help to calm a situation. Explaining calmly that you are there to help within your professional role, and that you are not there expressing a personal opinion, may help to keep the relationship within bounds and more stable.

CASE STUDY

Sheryl had worked for five years in a children's home and has had to deal with a range of aggressive behaviours by teenagers. She then went to work with adult offenders in the probation service. One of her clients, Jim, had managed to get a job. When he asked if their next appointment could be after work, Sheryl agreed and met him at the probation office. During the interview Jim became aggressive and threatening and Sheryl became afraid that she was going to be seriously assaulted. At this point she realised that no one else was on the premises, and that she had limited options for calling for help.

- What premises might have been safer to meet outside normal working hours?

- How might Sheryl make an opportunity to use her mobile phone?

- What other precautions might have been taken?

COMMENT

It is not possible to eliminate all possibility of harm. However, consider the task (is the interview likely to raise contentious topics?), what you know of the individual, and what might be done to get help prior to any interview.

ACTIVITY **3.1**

Personal vulnerability

- What sorts of insults have you coped with in the past, within work and in your personal life?

- What sort of verbal attack might lead to you feeling very hurt or defensive?

- What aspect of your personality or physique or circumstances is most vulnerable?

- What is your particular vulnerability?

- What can you do to mentally prepare yourself not to feel so hurt by a deliberately hurtful criticism in one of these areas?

COMMENT

Avoiding provocation if a client tries to play on your vulnerabilities is essential to competent professional practice. Prepare carefully for interviews through tuning-in and take time to reflect (alone or in supervision) on client interviews and incidents so that you grow through such personal vulnerabilities.

Manage your own non-verbal behaviour

- Respect the normal cultural space your client seems to require.

- Maintain normal cultural eye contact.

- Deliberately relax facial expression.

- Normally don't touch the person (at least not until signs of calmness).

- Maintain non-confrontational positioning.

- Keep your posture open but safe.

- Deliberately relax breathing and movements.

- Show receptivity through head movement.

- Keep gestures fluid and open.

- Normally don't mirror behaviours; this may lead you into reacting.

Listening and attending

Interpersonal skills for defusing aggression are an extension of basic interpersonal communication skills (Koprowska, 2008). It is often useful to express concern about the aggressor and his or her situation. Empathy with what he or she is facing can be tremendously helpful in defusing a volatile situation. Acknowledge that you have received the message (what the person is angry about) without getting hooked into a dialogue that is likely to damage your self-esteem. It may be helpful to remind the aggressor what he or she has to lose by continuing or escalating aggression.

As you begin to regain more control of a volatile situation, it may be appropriate to ask the aggressor to sit down to continue to talk with you. The change to a less confrontational body positioning will normally in itself help along the path towards defusing the aggressiveness. As with many human interactions, but particularly when seeking to defuse aggression, the tone and timing of any such suggestion is critical.

Assertiveness, energy and agreement

Some advocate adopting a similar pitch of energy in your speech as the aggressor, gradually toning down your energy as the aggressor does. You would probably want to pitch your energy just below that of the aggressor and continue to bring it down in parallel as the aggressor calms down. This is like the approach of a teacher needing to establish control in a noisy classroom. In deciding whether to use this approach you need to consider your relationship with the client, and whether this seems an appropriate mode of interaction to help to calm this individual.

Some advocate adopting assertiveness skills in dealing with aggression (see Bibby, 1994, ch17). Building your own self-esteem can be a great asset in dealing with such situations. It is said, and there is some research to confirm it, that children who learn martial arts are less likely to be bullied not because they win playground fights so much as because they do not present as a victim to potential bullies. Working through a training programme where you consider your personal boundaries and how you will deal with people who challenge them can be very helpful. Certainly there can be a place for explicitly requesting that the aggressive behaviour stop, and there is much value in learning to communicate honestly and yet sensitively about your feelings, the limits to your role and resources, and about the purpose of your involvement. However, there are some potentially violent situations where a less assertive and more placatory approach is more likely to avoid assault.

Approaches to defusing aggression

There are some more general pointers to defusing aggression. It is important that you maintain control of your own reactions. Your moral authority as a professional seeking to help the client will be undermined if you behave unprofessionally. You might refer to past strengths or achievements of the client and progress that has been made, particularly if current prospects look bleak. On rare occasions humour can be appropriate to defuse a tense situation. You could consider diverting the focus of attention, particularly if the situation is getting so serious that focusing on the real work and leaving aside personalities is not working. Do not forget that having the embarrassment of leaving prematurely is better than getting assaulted. You may find it useful to think in terms of distracting the person so as to make your escape.

ACTIVITY 3.2

Your experience of assault

- *What experience have you had of being assaulted or being a witness to an assault?*

- *How did you feel after the incident?*

- *How has it affected your attitudes and subsequent behaviour?*

- *Have you inflicted violence on others?*

- *If so, what issues have you had to face up to, and how have you changed?*

- *If you have unresolved issues about past violence seek help from a suitable counsellor.*

COMMENT

Past incidents of violence in your own life may have an effect on how you trust and behave with clients. Reflect on important incidents and discuss with a trusted friend or colleague how they might impact on your work.

Legal and ethical aspects of self-defence

As professionals we recognise that we have a moral as well as legal responsibility to respect the autonomy of our clients. Professional codes of practice for social work, as with other professions, contain valuable statements to guide practice, often emphasising the support and respect to be shown to clients. However, when a person is becoming aggressive and is potentially violent your priority is your own safety and the safety of others to avoid injury or death. This is rarely highlighted in professional codes but needs to be emphasised more often. Support for clients and help with their problems needs to be put in the context of mutual respect between the professional and the person seeking help.

The basic criterion for use of force to protect yourself is 'reasonableness'. A person may use such force as is reasonable in the circumstances as he honestly believes to be necessary to defend himself or another. Even where it is permissible to use force, it must always be within the criterion of reasonableness as determined by a court of law. In general, reasonable force is that which is no more than is necessary to accomplish the purpose for which it is allowed (Dimond, 1997). The force used must be actually proportionate to the harm it is intended to avoid. A person may use force to ward off an anticipated attack provided that it is imminent. However, this a grey area legally and if a threat of force could be expected to deter an attacker then it may be considered unreasonable to use actual force.

Self-defence is one of the legitimate reasons for using force or restricting the liberty of an individual (Hoggett, 1985). The law imposes a duty on a potential victim to retreat and escape, but recognises that this is not always possible. You can use reasonable force in self-defence. It might be considered reasonable to protect yourself with something you happen to be carrying (for example, keys or a can of deodorant). However, it is an offence to carry anything designed, adapted or intended to be a weapon. If you decide to defend yourself, be aware that your attacker may be stronger than you and may take what you are using in self-defence and use it against you (Criminal Law Act 1967, Section 3; Criminal Law Act (Northern Ireland) 1967).

The law allows you to use reasonable force to prevent crime, such as another person being assaulted. Use common sense as far as you are able in such a situation. Note that a third party intervening in a domestic dispute between people who know each other is very different from trying to protect someone from attack by a stranger. If you intervene in a fight between drunken friends, you may find that both parties turn on you.

Systems for physically managing violence

As indicated throughout this book, there are various approaches to avoiding assault, defusing aggression and engaging positively with people of all temperaments and in a variety of situations (Allen, 2002; DoH, 2003; Maden, 2007; Richter and Whittington, 2006; Simon and Tardiff, 2008; Royal College of Psychiatrists, 1998; Willis and Gillett, 2003). For situations where assault seems imminent, there are a number of systems that are in use in the UK which each embody a selection of physical techniques together with (in varying degrees) skills in avoiding assault and defusing aggression.

The early systematic development of systems for physically managing violence in the UK was the Control and Restraint (C&R) system developed by the Home Office in the early 1980s primarily for prison staff. The C&R system was adapted for use within special hospitals (Paterson et al., 1992) particularly to promote techniques that caused minimum pain. This scheme is known as Care and Responsibility and is widely used within health and social care with the whole range of client groups. The teaching on breaking away from being held is suitable for support staff such as those in reception or catering roles, as well as health and social care professionals. The additional training on restraint and relocation techniques is taught to teams from particular settings – such as psychiatric wards and learning disability facilities – where staff are taught to work together. An alternative version of C&R adapted by the originators Aiden Healy and Keith Mann called Control and Restraint General Services is now also widely used within health and social care settings. Various schemes for particular client groups have since been developed. Key points on the most popular schemes are given in Figure 3.1 together with links to further information.

In the event of assault

If you are attacked you must decide whether to defend yourself, which may put you at risk of further injury. In some cases it may not be possible to defend yourself. In either event you did not ask to be assaulted. It is not your fault and you did not deserve it.

In situations of serious assault you should talk to a trusted family member or friend as soon as possible, and to your line management as soon as you feel able to do so. You will need to discuss at some point the value of reporting the assault to the police. The police and counselling services have staff who are specially trained to work with victims of assaults. If you want to report an assault straightaway, whether you get medical help or go straight to the police, try not to wash or change your clothes as they may contain valuable forensic evidence. If you want to report the crime at a later date, you can also do this.

Incidents should be recorded on the client's file, and appropriate others notified, particularly if more than one aggressive or violent incident occurs. Files and computerised data systems should contain clear warnings for locum staff about known dangers presented by individuals based on previous behaviour. Aggressive behaviours that might be anticipated should be addressed in the care plan for the individual. Under health and safety legislation, having identified hazards that are a feature of your work (such as a client who has been violent), you and your employer are required to do everything reasonably practicable to protect people from (future) harm (HSE, 2010a,b).

Managing aggressive situations with clients can result in the sort of frayed emotions that can lead to a complaint whether or not it is justified. It is important that you have the support of your professional supervisor and line manager (as appropriate) for your actions. It is also important to have professional indemnity insurance cover, such as is provided by the British Association of Social Workers, in case you are sued.

Control and Restraint – General Services (C&R GS)

C&R involves the use of techniques which endeavour to contain violent or potentially violent situations in a safe manner. C&R involves a set of skills that enables a person to break away when being held involuntarily, and an additional group of skills that facilitate physical control of a person perpetrating an assault. C&R originated in the prison service and has since been adapted for use in special hospitals. The actual intervention techniques have been modified over time, and variant models such as C&R General Services have also emerged, a modified approach to C&R which endeavours to minimise pain compliance.

Aiden Healy, Home Farm, High Hutton, Huttons Ambo, York YO6 7HN
www.careconsultants.com.au/index.php
Scottish/Irish contact: Brodie Paterson, Lecturer, Department of Nursing and Midwifery, University of Sterling, Forth Valley Campus, Westburn Avenue, Falkirk FK1 5ST
www.nm.stir.ac.uk/people/brodie-paterson.php

Care and Responsibility Programme

Originating in training for staff in psychiatric hospitals, the Care and Responsibility method for breaking away from an assailant and for team restraint has been developed for all health and social care settings and for all staff whether professional, vocational or in supportive roles such as catering or cleaning. Care and Responsibility methods were pioneered by occupational therapist Bill Thorpe and his team at the Centre for Aggression Management at Ashworth Special Hospital. Bill Thorpe started researching methods of controlling aggression because he was unhappy with the prison-service model of using pain to restrain. He emphasised the need to work with patients so they were not lost through violent confrontation. He developed the idea of using the body's natural movement to limit aggression. That also meant looking at other non-verbal ways of defusing potentially violent situations.

Tom Swan, Ashworth Centre, Ashworth Hospital, Parkbourne, Maghull, Liverpool L31 1HW

Crisis, Aggression, Limitation and Management (CALM)

The Crisis, Aggression, Limitation and Management (CALM) model is an approach to aggression management that employs an ecological perspective which views aggression as an interaction between individual pathology and the environment. It promotes an approach to behavioural control based on the systematic analysis and assessment of the underpinning functions of behaviour and assumes that a whole organisation approach, involving policy development and staff support, will be a key determinant of safety. The CALM system is designed primarily for use with children and older people. This system has the advantages of integrating understanding of aggressive behaviour by children and older people. The main weakness for an employer is that it does not cover the full range of the social care workforce.

CALM Training Services Ltd, Elmbank Mill, The Charrier Menstrie, Clackmannanshire,
Scotland, FK11 7BU
www.calmtraining.co.uk

Strategies for Crisis Intervention and Prevention (SCIP)

Strategies for Crisis Intervention and Prevention (SCIP) is used most frequently in learning disability services but has a growing following in mental health services in the UK. It is designed to help staff in prevention and crisis management of aggressive, violent or self-injurious behaviour. The training emphasises assisting and teaching clients to maintain self-control, and for staff to engage in proactive and non-aversive methods of handling crises, firmly placing crisis management of challenging behaviour within positive care approaches. The physical interventions taught are characterised by non-infliction of pain and emphasise that people should not be taken out of natural body alignment. SCIP training places much greater emphasis on early intervention and on de-escalation than C&R, which primarily consists of a set of reactive techniques. This system has the advantages of integrating understanding of aggressive behaviour by people with learning disability and including material on blocking strikes. Weaknesses are that there can be limited coverage of breakaway and restraint techniques and that for an employer it requires a major investment for a small part of the workforce.

Kevin Bond, Mental Health Services Manager, Dacorum and St Albans, West Herts Community Health NHS Trust, Mental Health Services, 99 Waverly Road, St Albans, Hertfordshire, AL3 5TL
www.bangestonhall.net/our-staff/scip.php

Structured Communication in Prisons (SCIP)

Structured Communication in Prisons (SCIP) has been developed by the prison service as a guideline and set of tools to help overcome communication problems for staff and prisoners. The tools are not intended to be a replacement for professional judgements of risk. One of the tools is RECODE – a specialised version of SBAR (which is used in health and social care) to clarify and defuse potentially difficult exchanges.

Ministry of Justice: National Offender Management Programme publication: Structured Communication in Prisons: Tools for Prison Staff. Enquiries and comments to Dominic Taylor: *dominic.s.taylor@noms.gsi.gov.uk*

Therapeutic Crisis Intervention (TCI)

Therapeutic Crisis Intervention (TCI) is a highly structured training programme to increase the skills, knowledge and confidence of residential child care staff to respond to both the feelings and behaviour of children when they are upset, in crisis or at their most destructive. Built on crisis management, prevention and de-escalation theory, TCI is based on the premise that the successful resolution of a child's crisis is dependent on the adult's ability to respond in the most caring, therapeutic and developmentally appropriate manner possible. The TCI curriculum teaches strategies to interpret children's aggressive behaviours as an expression of needs, and motivates them to choose skills and behaviours which reduce the potential for their own counter-aggression. The training activities teach skills that allow staff to monitor their own level of arousal to aggression, to use active listening and other behaviour management techniques. These techniques have the potential to de-escalate a child's anger and frustration, and ultimately help the child gain self-control (Badlong et al., 1992). This system has the advantage of integrating teaching about violence by children into the courses. Weaknesses are that it includes little on breakaway techniques and that for an employer it requires a major training investment for a small part of the workforce.

Martha Holden, Senior Extension Associate, Family Life Development Centre, G-20 Van Rensselaer Hall, Ithaca, New York, 14853-4401 *http://child-abuse.com/rccp/*

Figure 3.1 Personal safety schemes for health and social care staff

Coping after an assault

Assaults and aggression are often experienced as sudden and unexpected. You may have no opportunity to prepare yourself mentally and may feel helpless and vulnerable. Despite the arbitrary nature of many assaults and aggressive incidents, social workers who experience them may blame themselves in some way for attracting the attack. *If only I had...* may be the spoken or unspoken words.

Such an experience may lead to stages of denial, withdrawal, confusion and fatigue before normal living and working are resumed. There can be a profound sense of loss of control over their own life and well-being, a loss of trust in God or other people, a loss of self-worth and a loss of trust in justice and fairness in the world. We may suffer from a loss of that sense that we are respected as worthy, decent people, not least because we have been trying to help those more in need at the time.

As a result of their emotional turmoil, professionals who are assaulted may want to insist on ceasing contact with the assailant, including discharge from the unit or facility. Their feelings may for a time be projected onto managers, colleagues or family. It is very important that appropriate practical and emotional support is provided when someone has been assaulted, whether within the employing body or through an external organisation. Information on suitable supportive bodies is given in the websites section below.

CHAPTER SUMMARY

This chapter has focused on helping social workers in any setting to keep themselves safe from assault. We have emphasised the need to be aware of danger in relation to the client, others and the environment and have given pointers towards avoiding harm in office interviews and home visits and defusing escalating aggression. We have summarised legal aspects of self-defence and given pointers regarding coping after an assault. We have mentioned the importance of learning breakaway techniques to escape from an assailant, the place of team training in restraint and outlined various models that integrate managing aggression with helping processes and therapeutic environments. Some key points include the following.

- Anticipate and recognise danger and take action to avoid it.

- Keep alert; be prepared mentally and physically.

- Keep calm and assess danger, thinking one step ahead.

- Emergencies require emergency action: head towards help; run; scream and shout as necessary.

- Your employer should have policies and procedures relating to personal safety, such as a lone-worker policy and a system for recording where you are when on home visits.

- You must make yourself familiar with the policies and procedures of your employer that relate to your personal safety and protecting the safety of other workers.

- Under health and safety legislation in the UK your employer has a duty to provide suitable personal safety training where assault might be anticipated as part of your work role, as is normally the case in social work given the high prevalence.

- Be proactive in asking what personal safety training is available. Attend!

- If no personal safety training is on offer, speak to your line manager or professional supervisor. If that fails to elicit a response within a suitable time frame, contact the appropriate training department or contact your professional body.

FURTHER READING

Braithwaite, R (2001) *Managing aggression*. London: Routledge.

This slim volume by an experienced social worker gives helpful pointers for professionals working with clients who may be aggressive or violent.

Dimond, B (1997) *Legal aspects of care in the community*. London: Macmillan Press.

A readable text on legal aspects of health and social care including trespass to the person and negligence.

Ford, K, Byrt, R and Dooher, J (2010) *Preventing and reducing aggression and violence in health and social care*. Keswick: M&K Publishing.

This is probably the most readable and scholarly recent book on the topic of aggression and violence directly relevant to social care.

Turnbull, J and Paterson, B (eds) (1999) *Aggression and violence: Approaches to effective management*. Hampshire: Macmillan.

This book contains valuable chapters on understanding and responding to aggression and violence, including an appraisal of various personal safety schemes.

WEBSITES

CareCall
http://carecall.co.uk/
info@carecall.co.uk

CareCall provides a counselling and support service for health and social care staff who are assaulted or suffering from work stress.

Health and Safety Executive in England
www.hse.gov.uk/index.htm

Health and Safety Executive in Wales
www.hse.gov.uk/welsh/

Health and Safety Executive in Scotland
www.hse.gov.uk/scotland/

Health and Safety Executive for Northern Ireland
www.hseni.gov.uk/

Health and Safety Executive Bookfinder
www.hsebooks.com/Books/default.asp

The Health and Safety Executives are the enforcing authorities for health and safety in a range of work situations including district councils, government departments, hospitals and nursing homes. The websites provide a wealth of attractive materials including details of legislation and current policy issues in support of their mission to prevent death, injury and ill health in the workplace.

Rape Crisis Support
www.rapecrisis.org.uk
Tel: 0845 122 1331

Victim Support
www.victimsupport.org.uk
Tel: 0845 303 0900

Chapter 4

Working in situations of domestic violence

Gerry Heery

ACHIEVING A SOCIAL WORK DEGREE

This chapter will help you to meet the following National Occupational Standards for Social Work in the UK including the following.
Key Role 1: Prepare for, and work with individuals, families, carers, groups and communities to assess their needs and circumstances.
Key Role 2: Plan, carry out, review and evaluate social work practice, with individuals, families, carers, groups, communities and other professionals.
Key Role 4: Manage risk to individuals, families, carers, groups, communities, self and colleagues.
Key Role 6: Demonstrate professional competence in social work practice.

It will also introduce you to the following academic standards as set out in the 2008 social work subject benchmark statement.
5.1.4 Social work theory.
5.1.5 The nature of social work practice.
5.5.4 Intervention and evaluation.
5.6 Communication skills.
5.8 Skill in personal and professional development.

Introduction

This chapter will focus on helping social work students operate ethically and effectively within situations in which domestic violence may be present. Over 25 years as a practice teacher supervising and supporting students across a range of settings: family and child care, learning disability, mental health, older people, residential childcare and juvenile and criminal justice, the issue of domestic violence has regularly appeared and in different ways. For example, the shock experienced by one student, empathising with an elderly recently widowed lady who informed her, with feeling, *To tell you the truth love, I'm glad to be rid of the old bastard – at times he made my life a living hell!* Another student on placement in a residential home had built up a good relationship with a young person in the unit. She was confused and distressed when the young person confided in her that the bruises inflicted on him had been carried out by his mother and not, as everyone had suspected, by his mother's latest partner. His mother was subjected to domestic violence from this person, but was also physically abusive to her son and had forced her son to say that cuts and scratch marks on his face had been inflicted by her partner. Finally, another student on placement in a rehabilitation unit was supporting a woman experiencing problems with alcohol. She found herself becoming angry and upset with the woman when she intimated that she was thinking about returning to her partner who had inflicted significant violence and abuse on her.

How should these student social workers have responded in such situations? What are the values needed to work positively and in an empowering way? What knowledge will help ensure the responses are appropriate? What approaches are needed to bring the value and knowledge foundations to life within the messy, complex world of domestic violence? In a chapter of this length it will not be possible to cover all aspects of domestic violence nor to provide detailed analyses of specialised domestic violence interventions. Neither will it deal with the specific skills necessary to respond to the denial, anger and aggression that workers engaging with situations of domestic violence will often encounter, as these will be covered in other chapters. Rather, it is intended to offer qualifying or new social workers coming into contact with domestic violence a greater understanding and awareness of the complex context and nature of domestic violence and to provide a basis for sensitive practice. To this end, this chapter will briefly consider a range of issues around the definition, extent, causes, associated risk factors and ways of responding to domestic violence and to review some of major research findings into these aspects of domestic violence (Natarajan, 2007). This material will be used to provide general guidance to social workers operating across different settings to help them in trying to understand and begin to respond to intimate violence within close relationships. It will also reflect on a student social worker's involvement with the family in the case study and provide a basis from which to begin to cope with the hidden nature and associated denial, minimisation and blaming which often accompany domestic violence.

Defining and measuring domestic violence

A range of terms have been used to refer to violence and abuse within close relationships, including domestic violence, domestic abuse, intimate violence, gender violence, family violence, etc. For the purposes of this chapter, while recognising the complexity of the subject, I will use the term 'domestic violence' to refer *to threatening behaviour, violence or abuse (psychological, physical, verbal, sexual, financial or emotional) by one person on another where they are or have been intimate partners or family members, irrespective of gender or sexual orientation* (DHSSPS, 2005). As such, it involves a wide range of behaviours that can have profound, immediate and long-term consequences involving physical, psychological and social effects.

Real challenges emerge when attempts are made to measure the phenomenon. *The variation in estimates of the extent of domestic violence is the modern metaphor of blind men touching and describing an elephant* (Gelles, 2000, pp798–799). Part of the difficulty relates to the continually changing range of terms and definitions used across the globe. Nevertheless, the studies that are available consistently indicate that there are high levels of general violence occurring within sexual and family relationships (Hague and Mullender, 2006; Jones, 2008).

RESEARCH SUMMARY

The extent of domestic violence in Britain

21 per cent of women experience at least one incident of non-sexual domestic threat of, or use of, force after their 16th birthday.

7 per cent experience a serious sexual assault at least once in their lifetime.

Approximately 2 per cent of men report being victims of domestic violence.

Over 12 million incidents of domestic and sexual violence occur each year in Britain (Walby and Allen, 2004).

Similar figures have also been recorded in other countries – see Coker et al., 2002; Schafer et al., 1998, for the international context; and Watson and Parsons, 2005, for Ireland.

To date the emphasis, particularly in large-scale research, has been on men's violence towards women and this has influenced how the problem has been understood. This inclination has limited the extent to which issues relating to domestic and sexual violence are addressed for both women and men. Gradually, however, prevalence studies are beginning to cover the extent of domestic and sexual violence among both men and women and this has led to other explanations emerging. Nevertheless, from my own experience of 20 years working within situations of domestic violence, and reviewing much of the research, I take the view that *male victimhood only emerges as looser definitions of violence are used* (Jones, 2008, p206) and there are dangers that it dilutes the reality that women remain more likely to experience severe and chronic levels of abuse. Even in those situations which are two-way or couple violence, *the effects and experience of violence may be different for men and women. For example, the same level of violence may be more detrimental or more frightening to women than to men.* (Natarajan, 2007). It should also be pointed out that gaps remain across a range of important areas including domestic violence within gay relationships and within particular ethnic groups, which further limit understanding of the phenomenon.

---

*ACTIVITY **4.1***

The extent of domestic violence

Think back to your own upbringing. What experiences did you have of domestic violence within your own family of origin, or within some of your relatives' or friends' families?

How have these affected you?

What is your view of the extent of domestic violence in your extended family, community and wider society?

How do you view the respective positions of women and men in relation to being victims of domestic violence?

What are the implications of your views for your practice?

COMMENT

> *As our awareness of domestic violence increases we may reframe our experiences in the light of this new conceptualisation. The widespread extend of aggressiveness in families by both men and women suggests that many more people have experienced domestic violence than verbalise it.*

Understanding and responding to domestic violence

In one sense *there are far more statistics about violence than there is knowledge* (Stanko, 2002, p42). A good starting point for anyone seeking to intervene in families and relationships where violence and abuse exist is from a position of humility in reaching a full understanding of it. Violence of any sort, and domestic violence in particular, is an enormously complex, multi-determined range of behaviours (Gilligan, 2000). A wide range of diverse explanations have been put forward in seeking to understand its causes and no single theory will ever explain the phenomenon fully. Biological, psychological and social perspectives have been brought to bear to highlight the multifaceted nature of domestic violence (Heery, 2000).

RESEARCH SUMMARY

Explanations of domestic violence: An ecological perspective

Biological and personal history	*psychological and personality disorders* *impulsivity and aggression*
Close relationships	*previous negative experiences in family of origin* *consequences of early relationships and unresolved conflict* *fatherless families (Miedzian,1992)*
Community context	*economic stress, unemployment and low educational achievement* *residential mobility*
Broad societal factors	*social and cultural norms* *male dominance and patriarchy* *relevant social policies*

(Adapted from World Health Organisation, 2004)

Domestic Violence is a complex phenomenon that demands explanation from a variety of perspectives (Natarajan, 2007, pxviii). There is a danger of an over-strict adherence to a particular theoretical approach or to an ideological view that may limit a full understanding of a particular individual's behaviour. The ecological model outlined in the research summary provides a useful framework within which various factors can be considered and also can show how factors at each level can be strengthened or modified by factors at another level. However, it also needs to be pointed out that within each of the levels, aspects of the research remain controversial and contested. For example, in relation to the impact of early life experiences, one longitudinal study indicated that witnessing parental violence and the experience of prior victimisation is a strong indicator of later violence and interestingly pointed out that this intergenerational transmission of violence is stronger for females (Mihalic and Elliot, 1997). However, the empirical evidence for the intergenerational concept of abuse has been challenged, and its determinate approach has been criticised as blocking awareness of alternatives that people do have, even if they have experienced abuse (Jenkins, 2010). Many young men who have experienced violence as children commit to being and in fact are non-violent (Mullender and Morley, 1994).

Research also supports feminist ideas and perspectives on masculinity and patriarchy as offering useful insights into the behavior of individuals. Domestic violence is viewed as a range of tactics, subtle and otherwise, used by various men to maintain their expectations, which have been influenced by processes of socialisation, about power and authority within their relationships. Many of the interventions that have been designed to help men address their use of such behaviour reflect this analysis of the problem and do have an, albeit limited, evidence basis (Dobash and Dobash, 2000). However, there is also the research, referred to in the summary above, which correlates the absence of positive father figures with future abusive behaviour. The complexity and messiness of the issue is also illustrated in a recent small-scale piece of research that sought out the views of women whose male partners were required to attend a criminal justice domestic violence programme because they had perpetrated violence on their partners. Not one woman conceptualised the violence they had faced with reference to an underlying 'gender power' philosophy (which was the basis of the approach of the programme), or made reference to such concepts as power, control or patriarchy. *Almost all the women, to varying degrees, understood the men's use of violence with reference to alcohol, early childhood abuse or the woman's own behaviour* (Madoc-Jones and Rosco, 2010, p161).

There is a need to work with a set of alternative interpretive frameworks rather than with a single-minded assumption that every case of violence fits the same pattern. This may allow for flexible and helpful responses to individual situations, needs and expectations, which are not being over-constrained by ideological perspectives or institutionalised procedures. In other words, in seeking to understand and respond to situations of domestic violence (whether it is in a heterosexual or same-sex relationship, or from a teenager towards his mother, or from a female relative of a man towards his partner, or as in the case study on page 58) the need is to connect social and cultural perspectives which may be influencing the perpetrator with the individual motivations, attitudes and behaviours that are playing out destructively within the situation (Jones, 2008).

ACTIVITY *4.2*

My understanding of why domestic violence occurs

What do you believe are the main significant causes of or reasons for domestic violence?

How important do you think it is to be able to understand why violence is happening?

How will this understanding impact on your practice?

Remember, reasons are not excuses.

COMMENT

It is important that our professional practice is based on sound research where this exists. You should ensure that you are knowledgeable about the risk factors to problems that are common in your field of practice. You will also develop your own way of conceptualising issues, that is, linking theories, research and your experience both at work and outside it. It is important that you are reflective and aware of the theoretical models that you use.

Risk issues

From the figures outlined on page 53, it is clear that domestic violence is a major public health and criminal justice issue that requires ongoing preventative and educational strategies to continually re-enforce the message of its unacceptability. It also clear from the extent of the problem that it will not be possible for social work services to respond to each and every one of the millions of domestic violence incidents that occur. The challenge remains as to how to identify those situations that require significant intervention. A recent large-scale study into domestic abuse in Ireland made a distinction between those experiencing severe abuse and minor incidents of abuse. It defined severe domestic abuse as *a pattern of physical, emotional or sexual behaviour between partners in an intimate relationship that causes, or risks causing, significant negative consequences for the person affected* (Watson and Parsons, 2005, p23). Clearly then, one of the issues and major challenges for any social worker engaging with situations of domestic violence, as we shall see in the case study, is being able to identify the likelihood of significant negative consequences occurring. To this end, research has identified certain factors that correlate with the potential for violence as outlined below.

RESEARCH SUMMARY

Factors commonly linked with a risk of further domestic violence in the research literature

- *Previous physical or sexual assaults (Walby and Myhill, 2000).*

- *An escalation in the frequency and severity of the violence (Websdale, 1999).*

- *Recent separation (Walby and Myhill, 2000).*

Continued

- *Either partner's attempts to kill or commit suicide (Websdale, 1999).*

- *Violence in pregnancy.*

- *The perpetrator's possessiveness, jealousy, stalking and psychological abuse of the victim.*

- *Previous criminality or abuse of court orders.*

- *The degree of isolation or vulnerability of the victim – women aged 16 to 24 years report more domestic violence (Walby and Myhill, 2000).*

- *Child abuse and previous contact with a child protection agency.*

- *Finally, mental disorder has also been identified as a risk factor for violence in both intimate relationships and other circumstances (Home Office, 2002).*

There is also the controversial issue as to how much weight should be given to the view of the victim in relation to assessing risk in domestic violence situations. Again, the research has tended to focus largely on females within heterosexual relationships. It has been argued that the predictions made by the victims of domestic violence must be more accurate because they have more contact, knowledge and history of the abuser than anyone else. They will be especially attuned to the warning signs of impending violence. On the other hand, there are several logical reasons why victims might make inaccurate predictions about the likelihood of further violence. They may have become desensitised because of their experience of past abuse and trauma (Campbell, 1995). They may have become so degraded and demoralised that they doubt their own judgement. They may fear the consequences if they are open about the reality of what is going on and may minimise the danger. One piece of research looking at this issue concluded that while predictions of domestic violence are most accurate using a combination of methods, including reference to the statistical-based risk factors outlined above as well as the workers' intuition, the victim's own prediction was the strongest correlate with future violence (Weisz et al., 2000).

While the above information will provide social workers, including students, with some understanding of the combination of factors that have been correlated with risk, they will not in themselves provide certain answers to the level of risk at a particular point within a specific situation (as in the case study below). The reality remains that *any assumption that people who are violent are similar to each other and different from non-violent people ... is fatally flawed* (Milner and Myers, 2007, p135). Risk assessment remains an inexact science or as Taylor (2010) notes, a highly fallible task. Similarly, Calder (2003) points out that it is difficult to develop any predictive instrument with a high degree of accuracy in child protection. Despite this, social workers are required to make risk assessments in a climate of high accountability and blame. Not surprisingly there is the danger of feeling pressurised to take a 'better safe than sorry' defensive position. From this may emerge an over-assessment of risk, risk-inflation and net-widening, with the consequent result that agencies over-intrude, focus resources too widely, and cannot adequately target genuinely high-risk cases (Pritchard and Kemshall, 1995). There is also the associated danger that an overestimation of risk may lead to some *women experiencing inappropriate and heavy handed interventions from child protection agencies* (Rowsell, 2003, p282). There is sometimes a fine line between seeking to empower a woman living in a situation of domestic violence and seeking to ensure the protection of children.

CASE STUDY

Jim and Mary; Part 1: The context

The situation with Mary and Jim and their three children has been deteriorating in the months since he lost his job. Even before this, the parental relationship had been volatile at times, particularly when they had both been drinking heavily. This would sometimes have seen simmering tensions and conflict between them erupt into verbal and physical abuse. Two-way shouting and screaming with some pushing, shoving and hitting would occasionally end up with Mary having some bruises. This caused both parties shame and embarrassment. They felt it was to do with too much alcohol and would usually try to reduce their intake after particularly bad outbursts of conflict. Fortunately, these incidents had been rare and with both of them working they were generally settled as a family unit and committed to their children. However, Jim found his protracted period of unemployment increasingly difficult. He became more and more aggressive within the home, particularly towards Mary but also to the children. On one occasion, he grabbed and forcibly held Mary when she intervened during an argument between him and his elder son. Jim was sullen and prone to sudden changes in mood and the family members felt they were walking on egg shells around him. On another occasion, after spending the day drinking with some friends, he became extremely threatening to Mary and the children, putting his fist through a bedroom door and threatening to kill her if she didn't stop 'fucking treating me like dirt'. He then grabbed her by the throat in the kitchen and pulled his right hand back in a fist as if to hit her. She was in fear for her safety and pushed him. He was intoxicated and stumbled, allowing her, with the help of her son, to break free and ring the police. The children were present in the house during this incident and the eldest son jumped in between his parents to protect his mother. The police arrested Jim but released him the next day when Mary indicated that she did not wish to press charges.

Shortly after the police report (which also confirmed that Jim had no previous convictions and that the police had never previously been called out to the house), but before anyone had contacted Jim and Mary, a further referral had been received from a health visitor. This indicated that Mary had disclosed that Jim was sometimes very controlling financially and emotionally. She also told the health visitor that Jim's mood would deteriorate every couple of months. During these times he was verbally abusive and said horrible things. This lasted for several days and there was a bad atmosphere in the home. After it, although Jim would be remorseful, Mary had a sense of the situation getting worse and getting out of control and she was worried how it might affect the children, and also herself, particularly as she was trying to get full-time work as a care helper. Mary reported to the health visitor that she could not discuss any of these issues when Jim was present.

While trying to make contact with Mary and Jim, the social worker also contacted the school and concerns were being expressed about the attendance and behaviour of the eldest child. His work had deteriorated and he was also becoming involved in aggressive outbursts towards other pupils and also one of the teachers in the school. The school had met with the parents to discuss the situation.

CASE STUDY

Jim and Mary; Part 2: First social work intervention

Eventually, when the social worker visited the home (Jim was not there as he said he had to go to the job centre at the time of the visit), Mary maintained that the situation was not as bad as she had told the health visitor. She stated that the police call-out had shocked Jim and he knew he couldn't get away with stuff like that again. A subsequent meeting with Jim and Mary was similar in tone with both insisting that the social worker was exaggerating the problem and that her interference was in fact causing more distress and upset to the whole family. The social worker also spent some time talking to the children who were generally guarded in what they said although their daughter did say that her parents were arguing and shouting a lot. She also told the social worker that her daddy had come in and struck her on the face when she was lying in her bed because she kept shouting and yelling at her brother who was teasing her. When this was subsequently put to Jim, he said that his daughter had been shouting and screaming at the top of her voice and was frightening the baby and he had just swiped his hand out at her, the blankets of the bed cushioned his blow and she was hardly touched.

ACTIVITY 4.3

What are your views about Jim and Mary's explanation of events?

Would you confront Jim directly? What would be your concerns if you did so?

What emotional reaction are you having in relation to the case so far?

What further information would you want to have?

In completing an initial assessment, the social worker was concerned that the experiences outlined above would be impacting negatively, both emotionally and psychologically, on Mary and the children. She was aware of a range of research linking domestic violence with childhood psychological disturbance such as depression, anxiety, PTSD symptoms, substance misuse and aggressive behavior (Humphreys and Stanley, 2006). She was also aware of the research that *consistently suggested that the most likely context to find child abuse is where domestic violence is present, and vice versa* (Rowsell, 2003, p282) She reflected on whether or not it was possible for an abusive partner to be a good father (Rakil, 2006). She also reflected on whether or not to instigate child protection investigations, and if the case crossed the threshold for intervention. She did feel strongly that the children were in need of some support services (Deveney, 2010).

Jim and Mary; Part 3: The case conference

Jim and Mary came to the initial case conference to discuss their situation. They were shocked by the content and tone of the social worker's report. Jim in particular felt that he was being made out as a monster and was angry and upset during the meeting, at one point standing up and stating: I can't take anymore of listening to this garbage, you haven't listened to a word I've said, there are kids in our street and their mothers are out fucking partying all night leaving them on their own and they're not getting fed and you are hounding us... *and then leaving the room. The meeting concluded that Jim would be asked to leave the family home for a period and Mary and the children would be offered support in relation to their experiences of aggression and abuse from Jim.*

Both Mary and Jim were upset and angry at this turn of events, particularly around Jim being asked to temporarily leave the family home, and move in with his parents. Mary objected to this, saying that it would make it difficult for her to go to her job as Jim had been able to mind the children for her and they didn't have to rely on her family members for childminding. They both expressed the view that the social worker was exaggerating the harm being caused to their children by aspects of their behaviour. However, they reluctantly agreed to the plan, which was aimed at addressing the effects of the violence, trying to ensure that it did not happen again and working towards Jim returning to the family unit.

Assessing risk

Reviewing the earlier material on risk, how would you judge whether or not this situation has crossed over the threshold into severe abuse and is causing real harm?

In terms of its severity, what are the risks of significant or lethal violence?

What is the impact of the violence on Mary, on the children, on the quality of parenting? What are the protective factors present in the situation?

How do you feel about the agreed plan?

How much weight would you give to Mary's views about how best to deal with the situation?

Professional judgements about whether or not to intervene in a situation of potential harm are often difficult. Situations might be appraised in terms of whether the main factors are above or below some decision threshold or by balancing up risk factors against protective factors (see Taylor, 2010). This is an area where further research is required.

The student's role

The student social worker had a limited role within the plan of work agreed at the initial case conference above. Specifically, she was tasked with monitoring some of the contacts between Jim and his children. She was also asked to contribute to the assessment of the children in terms of their views and feelings about their family life and the degree to which the violence that had been taking place within their family was impacting on them. She acknowledged a sense of fear and apprehension in engaging with Jim. She sought out and familiarised herself with the agency practice and procedures designed to keep her safe from violent and abusive behaviour, although she was not confident as to how helpful they would be. As well as her fear, she also recognised the need to be open about, manage and discharge the strong feelings of revulsion and disgust she experienced in relation to some aspects of Jim's behaviour. (She had personal experiences of domestic violence and worried how this would impact on her.) She initially baulked at the idea of working in an anti-oppressive way with someone who she felt was clearly oppressing the rights of his wife and children. How could she possibly maintain a commitment to work with him in a respectful, open and empowering way reflecting the social work codes of practice without minimising the risk that some of his behaviours presented? On another level she also experienced a sense of unease and ambiguity about her role. On the one hand, she was part of a team investigating potential abuse, occupying a powerful and potentially controlling position while simultaneously seeking to offer support and work in partnership with the family.

ACTIVITY **4.5**

Intervening in situations of domestic violence

What are your views about the ability of someone to be a good parent if they are violent and abusive to their partner?

How would you feel about engaging in contact with Jim during contact with his children?

What concerns would you have?

How do you feel you would manage any negative feelings you may have towards him?

What are your views and your feelings in relation to the power you have over this family?

How much weight would you give to the children's view of the situation?

COMMENT

One of the main challenges for the student social worker is often to gain the confidence to intervene in safeguarding situations while retaining some humility regarding the limits to our knowledge and our capacity to protect.

The opportunity for consideration of value, ethical and knowledge issues in relation to domestic violence was critical in helping the student face the challenge of going forward into professional practice with the various members of the family. She needed to connect professional practice and her growing knowledge with the situation at hand through the use of a wide range of skills. This is both a more extensive and a much more complex idea than just using evidence in practice (Fook, 2007). On the one hand, she needed to be clear and assertive with Jim and Mary as to her role and her commitment to seek to help address the difficulties that the family were experiencing. More specifically, she needed to work to make a meaningful connection with Jim. In her initial interactions with him, she wasn't sure if some of her negative feelings at times leaked out to him. In particular, the frustration and anger he expressed at times at the slowness of the process in allowing him to go back to his family annoyed her. However, on reflecting on this she was able to recognise many aspects of this behaviour as normal. Fear and anger will be experienced by nearly all parents at the thought of interference into their family life with the implicit threat of the removal of children very much to the fore of their minds. Those intervening with families in such situations must never lose touch with this reality and the awesome responsibility placed on them in making such intrusions into the private lives of families. The student was able to use some of the key skills in responding to anger explored in other chapters which helped, particularly in acknowledging and reflecting Jim's strong feelings back to him, but also seeking to connect with his own goals and hopes for his family. In particular, her growing ability to empathise in a genuine way with Jim's pain and frustration helped. She also affirmed positive aspects of his contacts with his children. At the same time the student also was more confident in encouraging Jim to work positively to address the concerns about his behaviour and its effects on his children.

The student noticed that as Jim engaged with the separate work focused on seeking to prevent the use of aggressive, controlling and violent behaviours within relationships, there was more of a sense of acceptance from him of at least some responsibility for the difficulties within the family. A recent national review of the literature concluded that, although controversial, work with individuals who are violent and aggressive is an important aspect of reducing domestic violence and its impact on children and young people (Worral et al., 2008). It is not possible here to go into depth with regard to the intervention with Jim, which was carried out by another social worker. It is vital that such work ensures that it *is both accountable to the man's experiences and needs and to the experiences and needs of those who have been harmed by the abuse* (Jenkins, 2009, p25). This was a message that the student sought to cling onto in her interactions with Jim.

Over the three months of her practice learning opportunity, the student also engaged with the children, seeking to build positive relationships with them and to give them the opportunity, if they wished, to tell their story about the domestic violence occurring within the family. *It is perfectly possible, provided communication is sensitive and age appropriate, to talk to children and young people about their experience of living with domestic violence and they have much to teach us* (Mullender, 2006, p66). The student was reassured by the contacts between the children and their father and was able to see that the children wanted him to return to the family home but not to be aggressive to their mother or them.

There were other areas of development for the student. Even at her level of responsibility, she realised that it was vital that she contributed to a multi-agency and team process in which information was being collected and thoroughly evaluated, decisions were recorded, and that any work carried out was within agency policies and procedures. On another level, in discussing the case with her practice teacher, who was also the social worker in the case, the student was impressed by the social worker's openness about and reflections on the decisions she had taken in the case and whether they were fair and appropriate. *Knowledge creation, through ongoing reflection on experience, is something that never stops in a committed practising professional at any level* (Fook, 2007, p372). Although clear about the use of assessment tools, procedures and related training, the student experienced how critical it was for the social worker to balance this with time for discussion and reflection.

ACTIVITY **4.6**

Learning summary

The opportunities for learning and development are significant within the contested arena of domestic violence. Reflect on the thoughts and feelings that have been triggered in you as the case study developed.

What are the values you need to embed into your practice?

What areas of knowledge and understanding of domestic violence do you need to continue to develop?

What are the key skills you wish to improve on in terms of bringing the above values and new knowledge to life?

COMMENT

Perhaps even more than in other aspects of practice, domestic violence can trigger personal emotional reactions among professionals. It is important to remain continually alert to such potential bias and potential inhibition to our capacity to help others most effectively.

CHAPTER SUMMARY

Complexity and uncertainty are at the heart of social work interventions within situations of domestic violence, and the social worker is often having to operate in situations of endemic denial, blaming, minimising and conflict. In this limited chapter it has not been possible to outline and do justice to all the areas of practice involved in engaging with a family experiencing domestic violence. It is also the case that a student would have a limited and protected role within such an intervention. Nevertheless, the chapter has explored significant elements of a challenging intervention into the lives of a family experiencing domestic violence. Relevant knowledge, including reference to a range of research, has been identified. The challenges involved for a qualifying student in accessing and relating this to practice have been outlined.

Continued

FURTHER READING

Horley, S (2000) *The charm syndrome*. London: Macmillan.

A personal and powerful account of the experience of domestic violence from a woman on the receiving end highlighting the often hidden, subtle and manipulative nature of behaviours designed to control.

Humphreys, C and Stanley, N (2006) *Domestic violence and child protection*. London: Jessica Kingsley.

This provides a useful review of the evidence base, policy and practice issues across a range of areas of domestic violence, focusing particularly on the needs of children. It contains both national and international examples of positive practice.

McWilliams, M and McKiernan, J (1993) *Bringing it out into the open: Domestic violence in Northern Ireland*. Belfast: HMSO.

A classic text and piece of research which brought to light the extent and nature of domestic violence being experienced by women in Northern Ireland that had largely been hidden behind the ongoing political and communal violence.

Milner, J and Myers, S (2007) *Working with violence*. London: Palgrave Macmillan.

A useful practice-based book which uses a case study to good effect. The complexities of working with violence are highlighted and guidance on application of a wide range of theoretical approaches in responding positively to violence is provided.

WEBSITES

Department of Health and Social Services and Public Safety Northern Ireland
www.dhsspsni.gov.uk
Tackling violence at home: A strategy for addressing domestic violence and abuse in Northern Ireland. DHSS&PS (2005)

Scottish Executive 2003
www.scotland.gov.uk
Preventing domestic abuse: A national strategy.

Home Office
www.homeoffice.gov.uk
Saving lives. Reducing harm. Protecting the public. An action plan for tackling violence (2008–2011) and *Call to end violence against women and girls* (Home Office, 2010)

Community Safety Unit Wales
www.wales.gov.uk
Tackling domestic abuse: The all Wales national strategy: a joint approach.

The four Home Countries have each adopted strong policies aimed at preventing and responding effectively to domestic violence. The websites above provide a wealth of information including national and international research, policy statements, strategies and details of legislation, in support of their aims to prevent and reduce the occurrences of domestic violence.

Chapter 5

'I don't want your help': Ambivalence and resistance in adult protection

Campbell Killick

Introduction

There is a growing recognition that social workers and other professionals have a key role safeguarding adults who are deemed unable to protect themselves. The vulnerability of specific groups within the population has been highlighted in shocking reports of institutional or domestic mistreatment. Policies and guidelines have been introduced defining abuse and the appropriate response (see David Gaylard's chapter 'Policy to practice' in Mantell and Scragg, 2008). However, the broad concepts of vulnerability and abuse are still not clearly understood. Our clients and their families do not always agree with professional perceptions of abuse and the most appropriate ways to respond. Social workers are faced with a dilemma, balancing the welfare and the wishes of vulnerable people in complex family situations. This chapter will discuss the issues faced by practitioners who meet with ambivalence and resistance when they try to support vulnerable adults and it will provide some pointers for good practice in this difficult area.

A problem of definition

One of the key problems for professionals protecting vulnerable adults from abuse relates to the definition of these most basic of terms. Early policies and procedures were imported from child protection, but it quickly became clear that the two issues were very different. There is general agreement among professionals and the public as to who children are and the acts that constitute child abuse. The population of 'vulnerable adults' is far more complex, relating to age, capacity, service provision and setting. The concept of adult abuse is not widely understood and there is evidence that professionals and clients perceive abuse in different ways. Processes to respond to abuse are professionally driven rather than client centred and groups representing adults have criticised policies and procedures as disempowering, resulting in a system that fails to meet their needs (DoH, 2009).

Welfare versus wishes

During the last 30 years the social work role with adults has undergone an important transformation. Concepts of support have largely given way to two separate themes of empowerment (or personalisation) and protection. There is an expanding social work role in protecting vulnerable adults from abuse and exploitation. Intervening in private family lives frequently involves resistance from clients and those who care for them. It is often the social worker's role to address sensitive issues in an environment that can be unfriendly or even hostile. Central to this issue are two questions.

1. What is best for the vulnerable person?

2. Who should be making decisions about the vulnerable person's life?

Figure 5.1 Understanding abuse, version 1

Our society generally presumes that adults are able to make decisions about their own lives. This concept of self-determination even applies when the person is being mistreated, e.g. domestic violence or criminal activity. It is only when people lack the capacity to look after themselves that the mistreatment becomes abuse. A graphic illustration of this is shown in Figure 5.1 and it suggests that the identification of vulnerable adults is relatively simple. However, the lines that demark both vulnerability and mistreatment are actually far from clear. This is because the definitions used are subjective, that is to say vulnerability and mistreatment are in the eyes of the beholder. To further complicate matters, vulnerability depends on context. Often individuals are deemed to be vulnerable because of the abuse that has occurred. A 70-year-old woman who has been living reasonably independently is made vulnerable when her home help starts to steal her pension money.

Figure 5.2 Understanding abuse, version 2

Perhaps Figure 5.2 is a more helpful illustration. The blurred lines around vulnerability and mistreatment intersect in a doubly blurred concept of abuse. It is possible that two professionals will have differing interpretations of this concept. It is equally possible that interpretations will differ between professionals and the people who they are tasked with protecting. Research suggests that perceptions about abuse are influenced by age, gender and cultural background.

CASE STUDY

Alison is a 28-year-old woman who has a learning disability. She lives in a supported residential unit with two other women. Alison works part-time in a clothes shop and she is also doing a course at the local further education college.

Alison has been in a relationship with Dave for the last year. Dave is 45 and he does not have a learning disability. Alison and Dave plan to get married in the summer but staff are concerned about her safety. Dave drinks heavily and has a history of violence. He often has parties at his flat that Alison attends and she sometimes stays over against her social worker's advice.

Last night the police were called to Dave's flat. Inside they found Alison, who had a black eye, bleeding lips and bruised ribs. Alison refused to go to hospital and she did not wish to make a complaint. She was adamant that it wasn't Dave's fault.

Alison's case illustrates the complexity and dilemmas at the heart of adult protection. An adult with the capacity to make an informed choice has the right to make decisions about where they live and who they live with, irrespective of the potential dangers. Equally, a person who is unable to protect themselves because of mental or physical incapacity has the right to be kept safe from the harmful actions of others. In supporting people like Alison, social workers and other professionals need to assess key aspects of the situation. There are two key questions.

1. Is this person able to make an informed decision about the relationship?

2. Is the person expressing their wishes free from the influence of others?

Both these questions involve scraping below the surface. Mantell and Clark (2008) have described how the capacity and understanding of vulnerable adults can be assessed. The social worker must establish if Alison understands the consequences of remaining with Dave. They must also ascertain whether her disability prevents her from making this type of decision. Thirdly and very importantly, the social worker needs to establish whether there are grounds to initiate an investigation against Alison's wishes.

ACTIVITY **5.1**

Imagine that you have been physically assaulted by a person that you love and trust.

- *What emotions might you be experiencing?*

- *What actions would you consider taking?*

- *Would you want to involve medical staff, police or social services?*

COMMENT

The above activity puts you in the shoes of an abuse victim. Perhaps the abusive act has made you feel angry and indignant. Your initial reaction may be to ring the police or pack your bags. It is equally possible that you feel scared, confused and alone. It is important to recognise that adult victims of abuse often make the choice not to avail themselves of support services. Some of the reasons for this may relate to the abuse itself. All forms of abuse have a psychological impact, victimising the individual and eroding their self-esteem. Explicit or unspoken threats can create a climate of fear and secrecy. In the period following a trauma it is difficult to make decisions that are logical, rational and unemotional. In a fight-or-flight response our hearts take charge and our heads are often relegated to the back seat. If you are prepared to allow professionals into your life at this time of crisis you might hope that they will provide protection and security. It is also likely that you will want them to proceed in a sensitive manner and at your pace. Perhaps you choose not to involve professionals and if they intervened you might choose not to co-operate with their investigation. In adult protection it is essential that practitioners understand the reasons why a victim might be reluctant to co-operate.

Reasons for victim resistance

As we have already seen, trauma is accompanied by a range of feelings and some reasons for resistance are directly related to the emotion of the abusive situation. Overwhelmed by fear and shame, the victim of abuse can feel powerless to change the course of events. Emotional and psychological victimisation accompany many types of abuse, particularly when the acts have occurred over a prolonged period of time. Emotional reasons for resistance include:

- powerlessness;

- fear of reprisal;

- shame;

- low feelings of self-worth.

It is also possible that a victim of abuse makes a conscious decision that professional intervention is not in their interests. They have weighed up the costs and benefits of reporting the situation and made the decision not to involve social services. Abuse is much more complex than criminal assault or theft by a stranger and often family dynamics play a key part in these decisions. Victims can feel a sense of family loyalty despite the abusive acts. Often they are reluctant to 'cause trouble' or to see a family member punished. A vulnerable person living with carers is in danger of losing their support if they report abuse. Like all adults, victims of abuse can fiercely guard their independence. Professional intervention can be perceived as a loss of control and victims may fear an even more harmful outcome. Vulnerable people are particularly fearful that they will be removed from the family home or lose contact with loved ones. Some practical reasons for resistance related to the individual are:

- family loyalty;

- fear of damaging relationships;

- dependence on a carer;

- distrust of police or social services;

- a desire for privacy;

- a desire to retain control.

CASE STUDY

Evelyn is 60 years of age and she has a history of severe depression. She lives alone and she rarely sees family or friends. Evelyn's teenage grandson Barry has started to visit occasionally. He is often intoxicated or high and he regularly takes small sums of money from her purse without her permission. Evelyn knows that Barry is stealing her money. She told the community psychiatric nurse (CPN) that she did not want any action to be taken.

It is possible that Alison and Evelyn would be prepared to discuss their thoughts and fears with a professional, particularly if they already know and trust them. If this is the case it would be helpful to take time to understand their perspective and make some initial assessment as to whether they are able to make an informed decision. Social work skills of engagement and empathy can assist in the building of a relationship which can then be used as the basis for information sharing and support.

In some cases obtaining the views of the victim can be much more complex. The individual may have limited understanding or communication. They may refuse to meet with a social worker or their carer may prevent access. Adult protection does not have specific legal powers to investigate and intervene. If there is evidence of harm or a criminal act it may be possible to use existing legislation, but otherwise social workers and other professionals find themselves with a duty to care but with little authority to effect change.

Reasons for carer and perpetrator resistance

We have seen the emotional impact that abuse might have on victims and discussed the ways that this might influence their behaviour. It is equally useful to understand some of the emotions and motivations of people who commit abusive acts. It is important to recognise that different forms of abuse have different motivations. The dynamics of abuse are complex but it is possible to categorise abusive acts as either theft, abuse of power and control or inability to cope. Financial abuse is an opportunistic crime based on the desire for personal gain. People involved in these forms of criminal behaviour often seek out vulnerable and powerless victims and they will endeavour to hide their activities to evade detection and punishment. Criminal acts should result in prosecution if sufficient evidence is available, but often professionals have the difficult role of protecting a vulnerable person when a conviction has not been achieved.

Controlling behaviour such as threats, extreme violence and sexual assault is motivated by the perpetrator's desire for power and it is usually conducted over a prolonged period of time. As in other forms of domestic violence, perpetrators may deny, minimise or justify their actions. They may also take deliberate steps to prevent the reporting or investigation of the abuse, which might include undermining the credibility of the victim. Professionals supporting vulnerable people in such situations may find themselves faced with similar controlling behaviour. Alternatively, the perpetrator may simply refuse to engage with support services.

The final category of abusive acts comprises those that result from the carer's inability to manage a stressful or distressing situation. As the vulnerable person's needs increase, the carer can feel trapped and overwhelmed by a caring role that they may not be confident or equipped to undertake. Rough handling, verbal abuse and neglect may be symptoms of carer stress or even burnout. The carer burden can exacerbate potential conflicts especially when there has been limited communication and warmth in the relationship. Carers in this type of situation may be aware of the levels of stress and the inappropriateness of their actions but they are not always willing to seek help. Avoidance and resistance may be a means for carers to cope with crisis.

ACTIVITY 5.2

Alan and Mabel White have been married for almost 70 years. Their children have left home and they now live alone in a two-bedroom terraced house near to the city centre. Mabel has dementia and she is becoming increasingly confused and distressed. Mabel does not sleep and she follows Alan around, repeatedly asking the same questions. Sometimes Mabel tries to leave the house and on two occasions she has been found wandering near to a busy road.

Continued

Alan's physical health is not good but he refuses to accept support in his caring role. He will not speak to any professionals other than his GP and a district nurse who visits Mabel each week. Social services have had reports that Alan sometimes shouts at Mabel and uses force to stop her going outside.

Yesterday, the district nurse visited the house and found Mabel to be cold and malnourished. She had bruises on both of her upper arms.

- *Who should be making decisions about Mabel's care?*

- *Does Alan have a right to be left alone?*

- *What would you do to ensure Mabel's well-being?*

COMMENT

Alan and Mable have been married for nearly 70 years and they have had a happy and loving life together. Their family life and privacy are protected by Article 8 of the Human Rights Act. We do not know Mabel's wishes or her level of understanding of the situation. However, there are very real concerns about her safety and her right to life is protected by Article 2 of the same act. Alan may have his wife's best interests at heart and he may be struggling with a difficult caring role given his own health problems. Skilled negotiation is required to engage with carers whose resistance may be linked to the reasons listed above. The social worker will need to show that their concern for Mabel's wellbeing is balanced with recognition of the positive role that Alan has played in her life. The initial objective is to identify a solution that satisfies all parties but Alan also needs to know that social services may intervene with, or without, his permission. The views and support of other professionals and agencies will be valuable at such a time ensuring that all possible resources are considered.

Good practice in dealing with ambivalence and resistance

We have seen that there may be good reasons why a vulnerable adult or their carer might be ambivalent or resistant to an abuse investigation. Whether the victim agrees to the intervention or not, similar good practice guidelines need to be adhered to. An approach that empowers victims and even perpetrators has the most potential to produce long-term benefits.

> **Policy brief**
>
> The Department of Health Guidelines *No Secrets (Department of Health, 2000)* describe eight principles for good practice that can be summarised as:
>
> (i) interagency working;
>
> (ii) empowerment of vulnerable adults;
>
> (iii) support for self-determination;
>
> (iv) recognising people who are unable to take their own decisions;
>
> (v) recognising that the right to self-determination can involve risk;
>
> (vi) ensuring the safety of vulnerable adults;
>
> (vii) ensuring that the individual concerned receives appropriate help and advice;
>
> (viii) ensuring that vulnerable adults receive the protection of the law.

If risk to a vulnerable adult has been identified or is suspected, action will need to be taken to ensure their wellbeing. The vulnerable person should be asked for permission to engage other agencies and professionals. In some occasions there will be no alternative than to proceed without the permission of the individual. There are two main options as below.

1. Investigating with the victim's agreement. Many investigations proceed with the explicit or implicit agreement of the victim. In some cases they will be eager to have the issue resolved; in others they will feel powerless to stop an enquiry process that they did not initiate. Irrespective of the victim's motivation it is essential that the process includes and empowers them. There is a danger that a procedurally driven response will fail to recognise the needs and wishes of the individual, resulting in secondary victimisation (Madigan and Gamble, 1991).

2. Investigating without the victim's agreement. If the individual does not have the capacity to understand the situation or if they or other vulnerable adults are at continued risk, it will be necessary to intervene even if they do not agree. This does not mean that their wishes cannot be heard, understood, recorded and where possible respected. Experience has shown that it is possible to include the individual in a way that limits the distress caused when we dispense with their consent.

Inter-agency partnership

The protection of adults and children within our communities is often perceived as a social services role, but effective investigation and support often require the involvement of other organisations. The importance of effective co-operation between agencies is highlighted in *No Secrets* (DoH, 2000) and good communication is particularly important when faced with resistance or hostility. Collaboration between social services, health, police and other key agencies is sometimes problematic but recent research (Reid et al., 2009; Manthorpe, 2010) suggests that a growing recognition of the importance of adult protection is promoting better information sharing. Increased formal and informal contact between professionals enhances their understanding of each other's roles. The combined knowledge of statutory and non-statutory agencies can be invaluable in understanding complex family dynamics and identifying supports appropriate to an individual's needs.

RESEARCH SUMMARY

There is a growing body of research in relation to adult protection, but surprisingly few studies have investigated the experience and perceptions of victims. Douglas (2005) provided a valuable insight into the experience and attitudes of vulnerable adults who had been abused. The victims interviewed recognised the need for intervention and they were able to identify positive elements. These included:

- *prompt responses;*

- *honesty;*

- *constructive engagement;*

- *practical support.*

However, Douglas found that many victims were ambivalent to the investigation process. He identified a recurrent theme that he described as procedure-initiated crisis, where the intervention compounds the distress and disempowerment felt by the victim. Douglas argued the need for a middle way of sensitive authority that recognised the needs and wishes of the victim while striving to ensure their safety and welfare. For Douglas, this middle ground presented a particular challenge for the practitioner.

> This is not work for the novice practitioner. It requires an approach which can both empathise and confront, can both enable and challenge and both support and protect.

> (Douglas, 2005, p41)

The skill of 'sensitive authority' described by Douglas recognises that in even the most contested cases there may be some areas of agreement. An understanding of these areas and the potential reasons for resistance assist the social worker in empathising with the abuse victim. Victims want the abuse to end. All human beings share a desire to be free from pain and distress and this is not dependent on their mental or physical capacity. Those individuals who have insight into the abuse will have wishes and views that they want to be taken into consideration. This is not to say that the client can veto any intervention but it is possible to ensure that their voice is heard and taken seriously. In some cases it may be possible to identify an advocate who will support the vulnerable person through the process and ensure that they can participate in decisions that are about them. Victims of abuse often feel in the dark about future options and they want information on available support and services. An informed individual is more able to choose a course of action that will benefit them.

Social services, in collaboration with other professions and agencies, can initiate a range of potential responses to abuse depending on the particular circumstances.

- *Prevention* involves the raising of awareness within communities about the potential for abuse. It may also involve the early identification of families where stresses or other risk factors are evident.

- *Preservation* models use a strengths-based approach, empowering the victim and building support rather than blaming the perpetrator. Similar to family group conferencing, this model draws together the resources within an extended family to break long-standing cycles of violence producing positive long-term outcomes.

- *Protection* is necessary where there is immediate risk or where preservation models would not be appropriate. In protection, social services control the process with or without the agreement of the victim.

- *Prosecution* is the legal response to abuse, showing that society does not tolerate the abuse of vulnerable people. In some cases action by the police and judiciary is effective in stopping abuse and protecting the vulnerable person and their property.

In practice two or more of these strategies are often pursued in parallel, ensuring the immediate well-being of the vulnerable person while strengthening the support network so that further abuse does not occur. As with all aspects of social work, good practice will be based on relationships, values, multidisciplinary communication and objectivity.

Working with perpetrators

As we have already seen, it is sometimes possible to reduce abusive behaviour and harm by intervening with the person who committed the abusive act. It is important to recognise that confronting an alleged perpetrator could put the victim or the worker in danger of actual harm. In addition, access to the vulnerable person may be lost or a carer may relinquish the caring role. Some clients recognise that their behaviour is harmful and this area of agreement can become the focus for intention. Some perpetrators are unwilling or unable to accept that there is a need for change

	Victim	Carer
Engage	Building relationships	Building relationships
Assess	Needs, strengths and risk	Needs, strengths and risk
Plan	Agree a course of action in relation to the abusive behaviour	Agree a course of action in relation to the carer burden
Act	Ensure safety and wellbeing	Addressing carer needs – alcohol, mental illness, isolation

Figure 5.3 Responding to abuse

As Figure 5.3 shows, the process for responding to abuse involves dual roles with the victim and the carer. It is helpful if these roles can be carried out by separate practitioners but often one professional finds themselves conducting both in parallel. At each stage the support of a multidisciplinary team ensures that all available knowledge and skills are utilised.

Engaging ambivalent or resistant victims and carers is difficult, requiring all the negotiation expertise that the practitioner has. The safety of the victim must be the foremost concern and levels of stress, fear and frustration may already be running high. Vulnerable people and their carers may simply refuse to participate. Raising the sensitive issue of abuse can spark immediate hostility. Transcript 1 provides an example of such an interview.

Transcript 1

SW   *Thank you for agreeing to see me Mr White. I have to tell you that I'm worried about the situation here with you and your wife.*

Mr W   *What situation?*

SW   *Well you're obviously not well yourself and I am not sure that you are able to care for Mabel any more.*

Mr W   *Are you saying that I can't cope? I have been looking after that woman for 50 years and I won't be stopping now.*

SW   *But your shouting and rough treatment are unacceptable.*

Mr W   *Who the hell are you to tell me how to care for my wife?*

SW   *Your not very well yourself Mr White and it may be time...*

Mr W   *My health is none of your business.*

SW   *Mr White, the District Nurse rang this morning to tell me that things aren't working. She also said that Mabel had bruises.*

Mr W   *That woman doesn't know what she is talking about.*

By the end of this short conversation Mr White and the social worker have had their worst fears confirmed. Mr White feels bullied and criticised and the social worker believes that Mr White is a difficult man who has the potential to be violent towards his wife and others. Lines have been drawn in the sand and battle is about to begin. In some cases there is no alternative to this type of struggle and social services will use the powers available to them to ensure the well-being of the vulnerable person.

The work of Douglas (see research summary on page 74) suggests that a middle way of sensitive authority may be a more effective means of engagement. Empathy allows the social worker to recognise the hopes and fears of the perpetrator even when their behaviour is unacceptable. This understanding of an individual's point of view can help in the search for areas of agreement.

Transcript 2

SW   *Thank you for agreeing to see me Mr White. How has Mabel been keeping?*

Mr W   *Mabel is keeping fine. I have been looking after that woman for 50 years and I won't be stopping now.*

SW   *50 years is a long time Mr White and it is clear that you are devoted to her.*

Mr W   *People are saying that I can't cope. I won't be letting some stranger take over now.*

SW   *I can see that you want what is best for Mabel.*

Mr W   *Yes I do.*

SW   *I would like to think that you will have a role caring for her well into the future.*

[Silence]

SW   *I'm sure that you are anxious about the future.*

Mr W   *We will be fine.*

SW   *Mr White, we both want Mabel to be as safe and comfortable and calm as she can be.*

Mr W   *I don't want your help.*

SW   *I understand your reluctance to bring in carers but I hope that you also understand that Mabel's safety is my number one priority.*

Mr W   *Was the nurse talking to you?*

SW   *Yes, she rang this morning.*

Once again the issue may not be resolved at the end of the interview but the relationship has been retained without the worker compromising on the key concern of Mabel's safety. Mr White feels that he has been treated like a human being and his views have been heard. There may be an outcome that is acceptable to both parties but it is also possible that no such agreement can be reached. In many cases the urgency of the risk limits the time for negotiation and relationship building.

> ### CHAPTER SUMMARY
>
> This chapter started by describing two separate concepts at the forefront of social services for adults. Personalisation prioritises choice and control while protection prioritises welfare. At first these seem to be diametrically opposed to each other but the chapter argues that good social work practice requires the pursuit of both. An empowering approach to protection requires the practitioner to recognise the complexity of family dynamics and to try to engage with the victim, the abuser and other key players in identifying a client-centred resolution.

FURTHER READING

Department of Health (2000) *No secrets: Guidance on developing and implementing multi-agency policies and procedures to protect vulnerable adults from abuse.* London: DoH.

National Assembly for Wales *In safe hands: Implementing adult protection procedures in Wales.* Cardiff: NAW.

Northern Ireland Regional Adult Protection Forum (2003) *Protocol for the joint investigation of alleged and suspected cases of abuse of vulnerable adults.* Belfast: Regional Adult Protection Forum.

The Adult Support and Protection Scotland Act (2007)

The above documents provide good practice guidance (or statutory powers in the case of Scotland) providing key definitions and promoting inter-agency co-operation.

Mantell, A and Scragg, T (2011) *Safeguarding adults in social work.* 2nd edition, Exeter: Learning Mattters.

This book provides a valuable summary of current legislation and policy. It also discusses good practice in working with victims, families and other agencies.

Nerenberg, L (2008) *Elder abuse prevention – Emerging trends and promising strategies.* New York: Springer.

This American book deals specifically with the abuse of older people, but it provides insight into the context of abuse, models to understand abuse and approaches to preventing abuse that can be generalised to other adult groups.

Chapter 6

Assessing the risk to children despite parental resistance

James Marshall

A C H I E V I N G   A   S O C I A L   W O R K   D E G R E E

This chapter will help you to meet the following National Occupational Standards for Social Work in the UK including the following.
Key Role 1: Prepare for, and work with individuals, families, carers, groups and communities to assess their needs and circumstances.
Key Role 2: Plan, carry out, review and evaluate social work practice, with individuals, families, carers, groups, communities and other professionals.
Key Role 4: Manage risk to individuals, families, carers, groups, communities, self and colleagues.
Key Role 6: Demonstrate professional competence in social work practice.

It will also introduce you to the following academic standards as set out in the 2008 social work subject benchmark statement.
5.1.2 The service delivery context.
5.1.3 Values and ethics.
5.5.1 Problem solving skills.
5.5.4 Intervention and evaluation.

Introduction

This chapter will introduce you to one of the most complex areas of social work practice, child protection work with children and families, and the even bigger challenge of engaging with parents (and other carers) who may be resistant or resentful of your involvement as a social worker in their family life. It could be argued that child protection social work is the one area of practice where aggression and threats to social workers may be quite prevalent (Littlechild, 2003). As the chapter title suggests, as a student or social worker you will have a primary professional responsibility to safeguard and promote the welfare of children and assess risks, despite possible barriers being placed in your way by parents.

Parental resistance and unwillingness to co-operate with a child protection investigation may be for understandable or legitimate reasons. They may have worries about the power and authority that social services and social workers have, and how they use those statutory powers to intervene in families. Parents may have a perception, usually not true in reality, that social workers are only interested in removing their children from their home if there is any suggestion of child abuse or neglect. This is rarely the case because the current child care legislation and policy that all social workers and other professionals work under, emphasises prevention and the need to keep families together, if at all possible (Children Act 1989, Children (NI) Order 1995, etc.).

But parents or carers may also be hostile and unco-operative if they have illegitimate reasons for being resistant to social work involvement in their children's lives. They may have actually abused or neglected your children and this may manifest itself in refusing access, covering up evidence, providing misleading information, using aggressive behaviour and threats to social work staff, and the misuse of the agency complaints procedure, all to hinder your legitimate investigations.

This chapter will develop some of these themes, and suggest strategies for how you can work in partnership with such resistant clients, while simultaneously staying focused on the social work intervention with your primary clients – the children and young people in the family. As part of this process there will be a discussion on the current family and child care assessment frameworks used in the UK. These are the Common Assessment Framework (CAF) in England and Wales, Understanding the Needs of Children in Northern Ireland (UNOCINI) in Northern Ireland, and the Integrated Assessment Framework (IAF) in Scotland. This chapter also provides some activities and research material that will assist you in understanding your practice role and function in assessing risk in child protection work despite parental resistance.

By the end of the chapter you should be able to:

- understand some of the challenges of working in partnership with service users in family and child care social work;

- consider the possible reasons for parents and carers (and perhaps children themselves) being resistant and obstinate towards you as a student/social worker;

- consider how to develop strategies for overcoming some of these resistance factors, while at the same time staying focused on your statutory responsibility of protecting children;

- evaluate the ethical and value issues associated with working with reluctant, and at times aggressive, parents or carers;

- review the issues for social work child protection practice following recent child abuse inquiries in the UK.

- *Spend some time considering a few legitimate reasons why parents/carers would present as angry and resistant when being investigated in relation to a child protection issue.*

- *Think about what you would say if the state (social workers and police) came to your door, or your relative's home, to undertake a child protection investigation.*

- *How could a social worker best undertake such an investigation to avoid antagonism and to work in partnership with you (if you were the parent)?*

COMMENT

You may find that you answer the questions differently if you imagine yourself as the client rather than the social worker. This approach is to be encouraged as it may tune you into working in partnership with parents and children, if at all possible. Remember, partnership in family and child care practice does not imply that the relationship will always be equal in relation to power differentials and the use of authority (see later in the chapter for some possible answers and suggestions).

Child protection in context

The tragic Baby P (Peter Connolly) case and the subsequent inquiry and reports (Laming, 2009; Munro, 2010), plus the subsequent trial of his mother and two others in the house, highlighted starkly the risks to children when parents and carers are deliberately deceptive and threatening to social workers. In jailing Ms Tracey Connolly (mother) for causing or allowing (with others) her son's death, Judge Kramer commented:

You are a manipulative and self-centred person, with a calculating side as well as a temper … Your conduct over the months prevented Peter from being seen by social services. You actively deceived the authorities … you acted selfishly because your priority was your relationship.

(Justice Stephen Kramer, 2009)

The review of child protection practice in England referred to as the Munro Review (2010), followed on from the work of the Social Work Task Force report (DoH and DCSF, 2009) and Lord Laming's reports into the Climbié Inquiry (2003). These addressed child death tragedies in the Haringey local authority and one of the findings was the challenges that social workers face in conducting assessments with parents and carers who are deliberately deceptive or manipulative when assessed by social services and other agencies. Their resistance can obscure key facts, distort social work perceptions, and in these cases make the social worker worried about their own safety when visiting such families. In Haringey, the Laming Report (2009) highlighted that the social worker and other professionals visiting were at times manipulated and distracted into concentrating on the needs of the mother (Tracey Connolly), rather than those of her four children, especially Baby P.

The demands on social work child protection services and the referral rates have certainly increased in light of the most recent high profile inquiries. The Munro Review (2010) mentions that there has been a *perceptible steep increase in referrals (11 per cent increase in the year 2009/10) since the tragic death of Peter Connolly* (p27). This figure was just for England but there have been corresponding increases in child protection activity and increased referrals in all the UK countries. These increased demands are being placed on a social work service that is already under considerable pressure to meet legal and policy requirements; see below.

RESEARCH SUMMARY

There are 11 million children (under 18 years old) in England alone and:

- *547,000 children referred to social services in 2008/9;*

- *607,000 children referred to social services in 2009/10 (an 11 per cent increase);*

- *only 6 per cent of all referrals were deemed to contain any actual or risk of significant harm.*

(Source: Munro, Review of Child Protection, 2010, p6)

COMMENT

The reader may wish to consider if these increased referral rates suggest there has been an 11 per cent increase in the actual abuse of children that is now being reported, or a more cautious approach to risk by referring agencies and staff (and the public), who are making the child care referrals.

This issue of what is referred and how it is referred can be very time-consuming for social workers in intake teams (know as Gateway teams in Northern Ireland), who have to make sense of referrals and complete initial risk or need assessments, usually within a short timeframe. In Northern Ireland the department responsible for social work, the Department of Health, Social Services and Public Safety (DHSSPS) produced guidance to assist staff in categorising and prioritising referrals made to social services, the *Thresholds for Intervention Guide* (DHSSPS, 2008). This is at a time when referrals are increasing in all jurisdictions and the demands on social work services are struggling to keep pace.

RESEARCH SUMMARY

Lord Laming's Progress report (2009) indicates increased demands on family and child care services, stating that:

- *200,000 children live in households where there is a known high-risk case of domestic abuse and violence;*

- *235,000 are children in need and in receipt of support from a local authority;*

- *60,000 are looked after by a local authority;*

- *37,000 are the subject of a care order;*

- *29,000 are the subject of a Child Protection Plan;*

- *1,300 are privately fostered;*

- *300 are in secure children's homes.*

(Laming, 2009)

The current political, procedural and legal context for child protection social work practice in the UK has been shaped by at least four decades of perceived failings, by social workers in particular, to protect vulnerable and abused children that were known to the agencies of the state (Parton et al., 1997; Munro, 2008). Current practice in family and child care in all the home countries is in the middle of another period of cyclical change, prompted by Professor Eileen Munro's review of the child protection system in England. Most other countries in the UK have audited their systems and procedures against the recommendations from the Laming reports (2003, 2009). This latest Munro review is a direct result of government criticism and media-fed, moral panic and public outrage that in the 2010s the state (and social workers in particular) seems to be unable to assess and intervene to protect some of the most vulnerable children in our society. This chapter will ask the question why this has been the case despite a number of decades of child death inquiries and reviews that produced similar themes.

If child protection is or has been everyone's responsibility (Department of Health, 1999) for some time now, and a multi-agency approach is mandated in all departmental safeguarding policies and procedures, then the frequent automatic blame attached to social workers in the UK when things go wrong may need further scrutiny. Is it the case that any social worker assessing child care standards can find this role very daunting and very uncertain, as parents and carers may have multiple needs themselves, and this can distort the assessment and the risks to children? It begs the question as to how this factor can be minimised in practice.

Can parents refuse to co-operate; what about legal powers?

Under the Human Rights Act 1998, article 8, it is enshrined that there is the *right to respect for private and family life* and this has to be considered in all child care practice. There is also a statutory (legal) responsibility for social workers, and indeed police officers, to investigate families if they have reasonable cause to suspect that a child in the family is suffering *or likely to suffer, significant harm* (Children Act 1989, Children Order 1995). This is the current legal threshold for state intervention in family life, but what constitutes 'significant harm' is not clearly defined in law (or indeed policy) and probably could never be because of the complex nature of the changing social phenomenon known as child abuse and neglect. Resistant and obstructive parents may be very aware of their rights, and if not, as a social worker, you are obliged to inform them of their human rights, but either way, they can easily thwart the efforts of the state to intervene to assess their family life (Cleaver et al., 1998; Parton, 1997).

ACTIVITY **6.2**

Consider the following statements and answer True or False if possible.

1. *Under the Human Rights Act 1998 parents have exclusive rights over their children. (True/False)*

2. *Social workers cannot intervene in families without parental permission. (True/False)*

3. *Social workers need a court order to gain access to a child. (True/False)*

4. *Children have to give consent to being assessed under the Children Act 1989 and similar legislation. (True/False)*

COMMENT

The legal position in relation to the state intervening in family life is quite complex in practice and competing needs and rights need to be considered; there is also extensive case law on these matters. In relation to question 1 about parental rights, under the current human rights and child care law the concept of parental responsibility is promoted more as opposed to rights. Social services can acquire this parental responsibility by obtaining some court orders under the Children Act 1989, etc. (but parents don't usually lose their parental responsibilities).

When social workers attempt to intervene in families they will usually try to do this in a voluntary manner, working in partnership capacity, if at all possible. But in relation to question 2 they can intervene, often in a time-limited sense, if they acquire court orders such as an emergency protection order (section 44) or a care order (section 31), under relevant legislation, the Children Act 1989, etc.

For question 3 the answer is usually true, unless parents give permission for voluntary contact and assessment. But if the social worker has reasonable cause to believe that a child in the family is suffering or likely to suffer significant harm, then they may apply to a family proceedings court for an order – see also answer to question 2. The police can also be used as they have police protection powers under child care legislation.

For question 4, children's rights in society have definitely been increased as a result of the Children Act 1989 (and similar legislation in other countries) and by the UK government endorsing the UN Convention on the Rights of the Child (1989). However, the issue of a child's consent for assessment is contingent on a number of issues, including the age and level of responsibility of the child, and again there is case law on this. Dependent on age, babies and very young children should not be involved in decisions beyond their intellect. Children normally have a right to be kept informed about what is happening and asked, if possible, what their opinion is of the assessment. A social worker will endeavour to get the child to agree to the assessment process but they can still proceed, when there is resistance, if there a child protection or risk issue, and sometimes this can be backed by a court order.

Assessing risks to children and unco-operative parents

The responsibility of assessing child care risks, intervening appropriately in dangerous families and successfully safeguarding children will usually be the biggest professional challenge that any new, or indeed experienced, social worker will undertake in their career. In child protection work the 'damned if you do, damned if you don't' dilemma has tended to permeate practice for a number of years (Cleveland, 1988; Reder et al., 1993; Munro, 2003). This phrase is usually referring to, on the one hand, an over-zealous, interventionist approach to investigating families, sometimes with flawed research and an inaccurate diagnosis of abuse (Department of Health, 1991; Cleveland Report, 1988), and on the other hand, a failure to intervene in families and remove children at real risk (Laming, 2003). This phrase has rather simplistically come to represent the biggest professional challenge that social work currently faces in the UK.

Anyone who has practised family and child care work will realise that by its very nature it involves working with uncertainty, and because of its multiple variables, assessing risk to children is always going to be more an art than a science. In practice, parents and carers are never or very rarely inclined to admit abusing, neglecting or injuring their children. Indeed they may deny, challenge and complain if any social worker or other professional suggests otherwise. They can use a range of measures to thwart any child protection investigation; see research summary on pages 91 and 92 (Cleaver et al., 1998).

The children themselves are often too young or can be intimidated by their abusers, so that they cannot seek help from any professionals or other significant adults in their lives. Child abuse is rarely just a medical diagnosis (Cleveland, 1988), and signs and indicators can obviously be missed; they can also be misinterpreted or confusing in terms of producing an accurate risk assessment (Corby, 1987). The various assessment frameworks, IAF, CAF and UNOCINI, used respectively in Scotland, England and Wales, and Northern Ireland, all provide a structure that looks at areas such as the child's general needs, parental capacity and strengths, and environmental factors and supports. They ask agencies and social workers to look at the risks and needs, strengths and deficits, within a family and its environs. But the completion of such an assessment framework, even when in some detail, with multi-agency input, has been shown to not always identify the real risky families in a caseload, nor do they in themselves provide for accurate risk assessment and good child protection planning (Parton, 1997; Laming, 2003; Munro, 2008).

All of the child care assessment formats and forms used by social workers, and indeed students on placement, were originally designed to produce time-limited, robust, evidence-based accurate assessments of family life. The process can be flawed in practice, and the outcomes compromised by *an over preoccupation with meeting timescales ... rather than the quality of that assessment and its impact on the safety of children and young people* (Munro, 2010). Although inquiry report hindsight can provide wonderful enlightenment, it can be argued that social workers have no motive to deliberately ignore obvious risky and abusive situations, unless they are incompetent and unprofessional. Instead, when assessing, social workers may find that the information they are analysing may be confusing or they may be being deliberately deceived (Laming, 2009; Munro, 2010). Child care assessments are always more complex in reality than the standard explanatory flowchart in the guidance. Child care practice is rarely just a matter of following the flowchart and procedures to uncover abuse or neglect.

ACTIVITY **6.3**

- *Consider some of the unacceptable reasons why parents/carers may deliberately present as obstructive, resistant and aggressive when their children are subject to a child protection investigation.*

- *Some parents may have mental health and substance misuse problems, or domestic violence may be a factor in the home. Does this excuse some of these resistant behaviours?*

- *Do you think that if the parents present as aggressive or resistant, this makes their children more at risk?*

- *How would you address the fact that the parents are exhibiting threatening and aggressive behaviour towards you?*

- *What could your own personal safety issues be?*

- *Could these safety issues affect your ability to do an accurate child protection assessment?*

COMMENT

All social work agencies and managers will have policies on health and safety, lone working, dealing with threats to staff, etc. Make sure you are familiar with these as part of your placement or work induction. Your own safety must be a priority also and normally social workers should be conducting a new child protection investigation in pairs or in conjunction with specially trained police officers, under a joint protocol type arrangement. In some longer-term cases, where children are for example subject to child protection plans or legal orders (care, supervision or interim orders), social workers may be visiting alone, but managers may well advise these social workers to also work in pairs if there is any suggestion of threats or intimidation. At any stage the police can be asked to assist in ensuring staff safety and to facilitate access to children, provided there is a legitimate reason.

Reasons for parental resistance

It is now worth reflecting back on Activity 6.3 and considering some other legitimate reasons why parents and carers may be resistant to social work intervention or assessment of their family life.

- The referral is malicious and there is no truth in the allegation. This does happen but social services are usually obliged to investigate all child protection allegations, even anonymous ones from the public, that on a few occasions prove to be fictitious.

- The client may have had a previous involvement with social workers that was not positively perceived; an example would be a previously looked after child who is now a parent.

- Concerns by a parent that social workers will remove their children from their care for no proper reason and uncertainty about their legal rights.

- Clients are embarrassed that their private family matters are now a public concern.

- Worries about confidentiality, and other agencies being contacted.

- Children themselves may have negative, preconceived ideas about social workers.

- The media may have influenced the view that all social workers are incompetent.

- The family think that they can deal with abuse within the immediate family themselves without social services involvement.

- Concerns about police involvement.

Ask the right questions, but get the wrong answers

Frequently as a social worker in family and child care services, as we have seen, you can be faced with parents and carers who mistrust social services and deliberately do not tell you the truth about their family life. From experience, for instance, parents will rarely disclose how much they abusing substances, levels of domestic violence in the home, or the final taboo – actions or thoughts that may endanger their children. In some cases the parents own upbringing, mental health issues or learning disability may substantially reduce parenting capacity, and the parents may have limited insight into the seriousness of the situation for their children.

As a social worker you are left having to second-guess the validity and reliability of the information you receive from the main carers or parents, and apply professional judgement to assess risk levels. The information from other professionals involved in the family may also be limited, out of date or conflicting in terms of perceived risk to the children. In fact the gaps in information may be more important than the actual information recorded on any assessment forms (Marshall, 2010). More important factors may emerge from the so-called 'common sense' approach to assessing reluctant clients. You may have to attach great significance to other concrete facts, such as why there was such a late presentation of an injured child to health services, discrepancy in the parents' accounts of what happened, or a family history of previous child care concerns. Social workers usually rely on other professionals to provide some accurate assessment (if possible) on areas such as the impact of mental health issues, substance misuse and domestic violence on parenting capacity.

ACTIVITY 6.4

A number of child abuse inquiries have found that the social workers and other professionals' fear of certain family members and carers have been contributory factors in diminishing the assessment and the protection of the child (Reder et al., 1993; Littlechild, 2003).

- *How would you assess reluctance and hostility; could you address this with parents?*

- *How may fear or anxiety be instilled in professionals visiting a home?*

- *What strategies could you employ to minimise the fear or anxiety?*

- *How could you ensure that the child's needs and any risks are still assessed to the best of your ability?*

COMMENT

The parents could present as very intimidating in their use of language, behaviour, keeping you at the door when you arrive, or using the presence of ferocious pets and animals to control your time in their home. The use of inappropriate sexual language and behaviour must also be considered intimidating, and discriminatory remarks made to social workers of a different race, culture or, in Northern Ireland religion, have been used as a means of undermining the professional.

In some instances, clients could feign co-operation, distract you from a focus on the child with their own life crises or initially ingratiate themselves to you as the social worker. But they may be passively aggressive and undermining your assessment in numerous ways, for example prompting the children on what to say to you. They could avoid you when you are trying to make contact, cancel appointments, make excuses, etc.

In all these instances the perceived intimidation or possible threats need to be addressed with the client as soon as possible. This may need to be done in an office interview, or the social workers could double up when doing these types of visits. As mentioned, most agencies now have a lone working policy and staff welfare and safety are of paramount importance. A clear verbal and written explanation of your role and function and any concerns you have can help to keep the assessment focused. Assessing the children outside of the home, if at all possible, can be invaluable in overcoming parental intimidation. Finally, good use of professional supervision will be important to help you identify and address any fears you may have about visiting a family.

Future challenges in assessing risk to children despite parental resistance

It would obviously be every social worker's nightmare (and a breach of their professional social care council code of practice) if they willingly ignored known risks to a child and, as a result, a child on their caseload or under their care, was injured or tragically killed. Even with the benefit of numerous earlier inquiries (Laming, 2003, 2009; DHSSPS, 2007) producing similar recommendations, the catalogued failings of some social workers involved in complex child abuse work appear to have become increasing difficult to explain. In examining what has gone wrong, this chapter has proposed that one possible under-reported factor may be how aggressive and resistant parents can undermine or disrupt good child-protection assessment practice (Littlechild, 2003).

There has been vehement criticism and ridicule in the media in the UK (incidentally this is not a worldwide phenomena) of how social workers appear unable to accurately predict which families and carers are dangerous to children and act appropriately to protect them. Lord Laming, chair of the Baby P (Peter Connolly) inquiry reports (2009), may provide some insight into how future social work practice should attempt to minimise the effects of client deception and intimidation on social workers. Lord Laming reminds us how devious and deceptive parents and carers who may have deliberately abused a child can be, and the lengths they will go to disguise what they have done. In Baby P's case his mother was deliberately deceptive in covering up her son's injuries with chocolate and creams when he was due to be seen by professionals, and she lied about her new aggressive and violent boyfriend, who was also convicted of causing Peter's death. Lord Laming commented:

> They become very clever at diverting attention away from what has happened to the child. Therefore people who work in this field – whether heath visitors, police officers, social workers, whatever – have to recognise this in their evidence gathering. They have to be sceptical; they have to be streetwise; they have to be courageous.

(Laming, 2009)

Immediately you can see the possible ethical practice dilemma for social workers who are tasked by legislation (Children Act 1989, Children (NI) Order 1995, etc.) and by policy such as Working Together to Safeguard Children (2006) England, and Co-operating to Safeguard Children (2003) in Northern Ireland, to ensure they work in partnership with parents in undertaking child protection assessments. This partnership working can rarely, and perhaps should rarely, be an equal relationship in terms of power and authority. While ethically and professionally social workers must strive to ensure that parents and indeed children are involved in the assessment as much as possible, there are times when the equality of the partnership must be restricted. For example, a father who is being investigated for alleged sexual abuse of his children may have his right to family life restricted during the assessment stage, while his right to a fair trial is upheld. Social workers and students have to retain a healthy scepticism about certain parents, as a few will be very dangerous to their children. Identifying these risky families on your caseload is not easy and asking to see the child's bedrooms, if there is food in cupboards, etc., as part of risk assessment can often test the partnership model but must be done.

As we have seen, these risky parents may present as overtly aggressive to social workers and other professionals in order to hinder a proper assessment, or a joint police investigation, of their children's care. On other occasions they may show disguised compliance and there may be a deliberate superficial co-operation with the authorities in order to reduce their concerns while concealing further child abuse. The challenge for social workers is to try to determine when parental resistance is for a legitimate reason and when it is a calculated distraction to avoid detection (Cleaver and Freeman, 1995).

What does research tell us to assist good practice?

The incidence and motivation of sexual offenders concealing their activities with children (Finkelhor, 1994) may be more readily understood than that of parents and carers in physical abuse and neglect cases that you are investigating (Brandon et al., 2008). The phrase 'believe the unbelievable' has never been more appropriate than when it comes to the investigation of child abuse. The challenge for many social workers is to come to terms with the fact that in all societies there are adults who will physically, sexually and emotionally abuse children, and grossly neglect them, when they are expected to be caring and nurturing. The recent public and media outcry over the Baby P case exemplifies the disgust, outrage and on some levels guilt that is felt by society when a child sadly dies after a short life of sadistic torture and abuse.

CASE STUDY

One case that shocked the UK and the social work profession was that of Victoria Climbié, who died in the intensive care unit of St Mary's Hospital, Paddington, on 25 February 2000, aged 8 years and 3 months. Her death was caused by multiple injuries arising from months of ill-treatment and abuse by her great aunt, Marie-Therese Kouao, and her great aunt's partner, Carl John Manning. Following their conviction for her murder, Lord Laming was appointed in April 2001 to chair an independent House of Commons statutory inquiry into the circumstances leading to and surrounding the death of Victoria Climbié, and to make recommendations as to how such an event may, as far as possible, be avoided in the future. The Report of the Inquiry by Lord Laming was published on 28 January 2003.

This report will make difficult, but essential, reading for you as a developing professional. It will raise issues about working with deceptive and resistant parents, relatives and carers. It should raise issues in relation to cultural identity and race – Victoria was a French-speaking child originally from the Ivory Coast, but illegally taken into the UK by her great aunt. If she had been a white, English-speaking child, would she have received a more robust service from all the professionals involved in her life? You might consider if the professionals involved, medical, police and social workers, were prepared in their training to believe the unbelievable.

Back at her great aunt's house Victoria continued to be forced to sleep in the bath, and was tied up inside a black plastic sack. As a result Victoria spent long periods lying in

Continued

---

her own urine and faeces. The sack ceased to be used when Victoria's skin condition became so damaged that Manning said they were concerned that undue questions would be asked.

By the beginning of 2000 Victoria was being given her food on a piece of plastic in the bathroom. Her hands were tied with masking tape and she would be pushed towards the food to eat it like a dog. Victoria was also beaten regularly by Manning and Kouao. Manning later reported that Kouao struck Victoria on a daily basis, using various implements including a shoe, a coat hanger, a wooden spoon and a hammer. Victoria's blood was found on the walls of the flat, on Manning's football boots and trainers. He also admitted to beating Victoria with a bicycle chain.

This case study is not unique in documenting the cruelty and abuse that unfortunately some children experience in our society. The responsibility to assess, intervene and remove children to protect them is an onerous one, but it is a key role for social workers and other professionals involved in such cases.

(House of Commons, Health Committee Report: The Victoria Climbié Inquiry Report, 2003)

In child protection the stakes are high and you must not be complacent or naive in undertaking risk assessments of potential child abuse cases when using the existing assessment frameworks. The completion of the assessment forms, in themselves, will not protect children, so remember these assessment frameworks are fallible processes, and finding time to make sound, professional practice judgements is just as important as the paperwork (Munro, 2008).

Factors that can contribute to an accurate assessment of the risk of child abuse

In a comprehensive review of child protection research and social work involvement, Cleaver et al. (1998) summarised the factors that can contribute to an accurate assessment of the risk of child abuse. These included the following.

- *The issue of the social worker's own safety, with instances of aggression or inappropriate sexual behaviour towards them affecting their ability to assess due to their own anxieties.*

- *The rule of optimism, where social workers who had been working with a family for a period of time overestimate the level of progress made, make decisions based on opinion rather than fact, or too readily accept parental explanations for injuries, etc.*

- *Similarly, over-involvement in a case can lead to a loss of objectivity. Failure to act on warning signs because of fear, stress or burnout.*

Continued

RESEARCH SUMMARY continued

- *Poor communication between professionals involved in child protection cases. Concerns about confidentiality and a lack of professional consensus on what constitutes risk can affect the assessment.*

- *Failure to focus on the child: the child's needs and risks become caught up in the overall family problems, cultural norms and other societal issues, which can distort judgement on what is good-enough parenting.*

- *Assuming that biological parents have a natural love for their children or are incapable of abusing or neglecting them.*

- *Social workers deciding the level of risk early in their involvement with a family, and failing to review or adjust this hypothesis when faced with new or conflicting information.*

As can be seen from the research and inquiry recommendations, social workers and others need to keep their crucial judgements on thresholds of significant harm under constant critical review. Indeed as mentioned, the gaps in our assessment information may be as important as the verified information gleaned from multi-agency checks and self-reports from parents and perhaps children themselves. A sceptical mind, knowledge of evidence-based child abuse research, good professional supervision, and sound professional analysis and judgement can help you in undertaking accurate risk assessments. The single most important factor in minimising errors is to admit that you may be wrong (Munro, 2008).

CHAPTER SUMMARY

This chapter highlighted the issues for students and qualified social workers in assessing risk and protecting children when faced with parents and carers who may be deliberately obstructive, resistant, and in the worst-case scenario, intimidating and aggressive towards you. The current legal status and policy for child care practice in the UK, including recent child death inquiry findings, have been reviewed and critically analysed. Possible legitimate and illegitimate reasons for this parental resistance have been examined and examples of how this may be manifested in practice listed.

The possible impact of this aggression and resistance on your ability to safely assess the risks to children in families has been discussed, and strategies for minimising this have been suggested. The use of the current assessment frameworks has been reviewed and the challenges of achieving an accurate child protection risk assessment highlighted.

Cleaver, H, Wattam, C and Cawson, P (1998) *Assessing risk in child protection*. London: NSPCC.

This research reviewed a large number of child deaths where social services had previous involvement with the families.

Laming, L (2009) *The protection of children in England: A progress report*. London: Stationery Office.

This report and its recommendations followed on from the Baby P (Peter) child death inquiry in Haringey.

Littlechild, B (2003) Working with aggressive and violent parents in child protection. *Social Work Practice*, 15 (1), 47–59.

A short practical review of some research on how resistance and aggression can manifest itself in practice.

Munro, E (2010) *The Munro review of child protection, Part one: A systems analysis*. Department of Education; available at www.education.gov.uk/munroreview/

This is the most recent review of child protection services in England but the issues being addressed are common to all the home countries.

Chapter 7

Working with irrationality and dangerousness in mental health

Roger Manktelow

A C H I E V I N G   A   S O C I A L   W O R K   D E G R E E

This chapter will help you to meet the following National Occupational Standards for Social Work in the UK including the following.

Key Role 2: Plan, carry out, review and evaluate social work practice, with individuals, families, carers, groups, communities and other professionals.

Key Role 4: Manage risk to individuals, families, carers, groups, communities, self and colleagues.

Key Role 6: Demonstrate professional competence in social work practice.

It will also introduce you to the following academic standards as set out in the 2008 social work subject benchmark statement.

5.1.4 Social work theory.

5.1.5 The nature of social work practice.

5.5.4 Intervention and evaluation.

5.6 Communication skills.

5.8 Skill in personal and professional development.

Introduction

In the book so far you have been introduced to the knowledge and skills needed to work with clients who feel angry and who may act aggressively. This chapter seeks to introduce a cautionary note in recognising that there are situations which are not directly amenable to conflict management and mediation. Such dangerous behaviours may be encountered in relation to people suffering enduring mental illnesses and may occur in family settings placing relatives and carers at the front line of risk. In a study of violence and aggression committed by people hospitalised with mental illness, it was found that the majority of violence involved minor aggressive acts, such as throwing an object, pushing, grabbing or shoving, and involved close relationships in home environments, with alcohol a regular feature and during routine activities such as mealtimes (Monahan et al., 2001).

RESEARCH SUMMARY

The MacArthur violence risk assessment study

The study involved the interviewing of 1,000 American psychiatric patients in hospital and during the first year after discharge to establish the risk factors associated with physical violence towards others in the community by ex-patients. Chief findings were as follows.

- *In a 20-week follow-up period 18.7 per cent of discharged patients were involved in violent altercations which resulted in police contact.*

- *Patients with personality disorder were most likely to commit offences.*

- *Compared to the general population, patients were more likely to commit offences at home.*

- *Ex-patients who abused drugs and alcohol committed more violent acts.*

(Monaham et al., (2001)

RESEARCH SUMMARY

Gender, violence and mental illness

Nicky Stanley (2004), in her analysis of women and mental health inquiries, found that:

- *some 20 per cent of homicides by mental health service users are committed by females;*

- *mental health inquiries underestimate the likelihood of violence being committed by female service users;*

- *females are most likely to be victims in their roles as carers, partners and family members.*

It is not the purpose of this chapter to reinforce the stigma of fear towards people with mental illness as violent and aggressive. Research studies of public attitudes to mental illness have found that, while public attitudes are now more benign and accepting than in the past, the public's fear of violence by people with mental illness has actually increased (Monahan et al., 2001). Rather we are concerned to provide the concepts to enable us to understand and analyse the components of such behaviours, which enable us to competently assess the severity of risk and act accordingly.

This chapter will also review the inquiries into tragic deaths committed by people with mental illness and recommendations as to how such tragedies might be avoided. In the final part of the chapter, the interpersonal skills needed to work with people with enduring mental illness in risk situations will be identified and described.

In order to be an empathic and effective practitioner we need to understand what it is like to be mentally ill from the viewpoint of the sufferer, and this experience is first described.

CASE STUDY

An early research study by the author involved the collection and phenomenological analysis of patients' own accounts of the events leading to hospitalisation (Manktelow, 1994). Here is such an account which demonstrates the kind of behaviours involved.

Alan is a family man living on long-term unemployment benefit. Out of the blue, he buys a van using his life-savings and starts a mobile shop. His new business does not flourish and fails after a brawl with a customer. In the fight, Alan suffers a bang to his head. Back at home, he acts oddly – talking of hearing the voice of his long-dead father. Alan wrote notes on his wife and children. When his wife questioned his note-taking, Alan became angry and justified his behaviour with the explanation just testing them. *His wife hid their father's odd behaviour from the children. Alan went out a good deal, drinking heavily, spending recklessly and on one reported occasion tearing up his money. His wife began to accompany him in the hope of controlling his excesses. Dramatically, Alan's behaviour changed to the other extreme – he couldn't eat, couldn't sleep and lost weight. His wife cooked special meals for him but one night he accused her of not telling him that their children were dead. At dinner, he threw his meal across the room. His wife escaped to a neighbour's house and rang for the doctor, who arranged compulsory admission to psychiatric hospital.*

Personality characteristics

Certain personality traits or characteristics are associated with people prone to anger and aggression. These include frustration, hostility, poor empathy and irritability. In extreme cases, these might constitute an anti-social or psychopathic personality. The legal definition of a psychopathic disorder is *a persistent disorder or disability of the mind which results in abnormally aggressive or seriously irresponsible behaviour* (Section 1(2), Mental Health Act 1983). Key personality characteristics are a pronounced tendency to blame others rather than themselves for their misfortunes, a masked dependence and an intolerance of being alone.

ACTIVITY 7.1

In the film One Flew over the Cuckoo's Nest, *Jack Nicholson plays a psychiatric patient with a psychopathic personality disorder. Watch this film and answer the following questions.*

- *What are the possible causes of Jack Nicholson's character's violent behaviour?*

- *What are the triggers to this aggression?*

- *How might this violent behaviour be prevented?*

This film is based on the book of the same name by Ken Kesey, which is a classic of the 1960s' counter-culture. It actually describes what was considered at that time a progressive psychiatric regime.

Psychiatric diagnosis

Although psychiatric diagnoses have been criticised for being a form of labelling and for their unreliability, nevertheless they are important for identifying discrete and identifiable constellations of behaviour. For example, a person with anxiety will behave in a markedly different way to a person with senile dementia. In the same way, the likelihood of violent and aggressive behaviour also differs between diagnoses. People with schizophrenia are more likely to experience hallucinations and delusions, and to behave irrationally as a result. As we have seen above, people with anti-social or psychopathic disorder have poor self-control, fail to appreciate the effects of their actions on others and act impulsively and aggressively. On the other hand, a depressed person is much more likely to commit harm to themselves than to others.

Gould (2001) draws attention to those severe situations when sufferers with extreme feelings of hopelessness may also feel that their loved ones are 'too good for this terrible world' and commit familicide. Puerperal psychosis is a particular form of delusion occurring in one in 200 new births during the first two weeks following childbirth. The mother develops delusions around the baby and there is a high risk of harm to the new baby and self-harm to the mother.

Dangerousness

The concept of dangerousness has been recently adopted, particularly in forensic psychiatry, to describe individuals who possess a significant likelihood of committing acts of violence on others. Mental health legislation identifies risk in terms of the likelihood of an act of significant physical harm to oneself or others. The concept of dangerousness widens our focus to the personality characteristics, the situational factors and the psychiatric symptomology of the potential perpetrator.

Impulsivity is a component of dangerousness. It describes the failure to only act after consideration of the consequences of our chosen course of action. The psychological term 'locus of control' is used to analyse the degree to which we own our actions. Individuals who act impulsively are difficult to assess because there are no advance warnings or signs about their impending behaviour.

Annual figures of the rates of suicide and homicide in England and Wales are kept and analysed in the National Confidential Inquiry into Suicide and Homicide. Approximately 10 per cent of homicides annually are committed by people who had contact with mental health services in the previous 12 months, with the most common diagnosis being schizophrenia. Victims were more likely to be family members, friends and acquaintances rather than strangers.

Irrationality

People with severe mental illnesses experience delusions and hallucinations. Delusions are false beliefs which are not amenable to reason. Sometimes such delusions form a delusional framework with a master delusion and secondary delusions. Hallucinations are imaginary sensory experiences which are experienced as real. Hearing voices is the most frequent hallucinatory experience. Such voices may be benign or non-threatening but more often may be critical and persecutory. Particular types of delusions carry a high risk of violence. These are known as command and threat overdrives. They are characterised by the sufferer being taken over by a voice or belief which they cannot control and which requires them to act against others.

Gould (2001) has drawn attention to the key factors which alert us to the possibility of dangerous behaviour by people with mental health problems. Firstly, if mental illness exists alongside substance misuse (what is known as dual diagnosis) then the disinhibiting effects of alcohol and drugs are likely to reduce internalised self-controls which may have prevented an individual acting on their delusional beliefs. Secondly, the nature of the delusional belief is crucial: if a person believes that they are being controlled by a force which they must obey and cannot resist (known as a command hallucination), then there is a heightened risk of violence. Thirdly, this likelihood is further increased if the individual suffers from paranoid delusion in which he or she believes that others are persecuting them or putting them in danger.

The condition of morbid jealousy or erotomania carries a high degree of risk of domestic violence and danger to female partners. In this case, the male partner develops a fixed irrational belief about their partner's infidelity and insists on monitoring, supervising and interrogating her about her life and behaviour. Such seriously paranoid individuals may otherwise appear perfectly rational and therefore pose a high risk.

ACTIVITY **7.2**

Watch Russell Crowe play an economics professor who suffers from schizophrenia in the film A Beautiful Mind.

- *Describe the delusional system from which Russell Crowe's character suffers.*

- *Identify the primary and secondary delusions.*

- *Observe how the character acts upon them.*

- *Identify situations of risk and danger to self and others.*

COMMENT

This film describes the schizophrenic breakdown of an eminent maths professor in an American Ivy League university. His hallucinations and delusions and their impact on himself, his work and his family are portrayed very powerfully.

Assessment of risk

Social workers take decisions of great magnitude in situations of uncertainty. This is the essence of being a professional and this is why professional training is so important. There can be no such thing as perfect knowledge and infallibility when it comes to human behaviour. But neither should we as professionals simply use intuition based on experience. Rather, as Taylor (2010) has recommended, we should rely on both clinical judgement arising from our practice experience wisdom and proven measures of assessment. However, it is worth cautioning that tools measuring the likelihood of violent behaviour among samples of institutionalised populations reviewed by Monahan et al. (2001) had a low predictive accuracy and prompted the researchers to engage in a major exercise to produce a new risk assessment measure.

Inquiries

Since 1994, in response to something of a public and media panic about violence and mental illness, inquiries into homicides committed by people with mental health problems were made mandatory. In a review of the findings of these mental health homicide inquiries, McCullough and Parker (2004) identified the following 12 key issues.

1. *Poor risk management* – either inadequate or absent. Recommendations were made for improved record keeping, staff training and the integration of risk management with care planning.

2. *Communication problems* – a failure to pass on key information in the right form, at the right time, to the right person.

3. *Inadequate care planning* – discharge from hospital was often premature and haphazard and the Care Programme Approach was often not used effectively.

4. *Lack of inter-agency working* – a frequent concern across all agencies, police, housing, independent sector as well as health and social care.

5. *Procedural failures* – both administrative and legal.

6. *Lack of suitable accommodation* – range of required accommodation often absent.

7. *Resources* – inadequate, poor quality and staff under great pressure.

8. *Substance misuse* – present to a greater or lesser degree in a number of homicides.

9. *Non-compliance with medication* – the authors feel that its relevance may have been overstated in some inquiry reports.

10. *Involvement of carers* – a worrying lack of involvement reported.

11. *Ethnic minority issues* – staff may have been too ready to make stereotypical assumptions.

12. *The need for reform* – a need to reform policy and legislation highlighted.

Assertive outreach teams are now seen as an effective method of intervention in response to the compliance and safety issue providing a comprehensive and balanced system of intensive community care.

The skills of working with people with severe mental illness

Mental illnesses are global in their impact on our sense of self, affecting emotions, thoughts, judgements and behaviours. The experience of being mentally ill is often one in which common human emotions are overwhelming and incapacitating, such as the feelings of hopelessness in depression. Alternatively, there may be an absence of emotion and warmth. This blunting of affect requires the worker to give more of self in their interaction with the sufferer, which workers must acknowledge can be a draining experience. In some cases, emotions may fluctuate between extremes of well-being and despair, which causes an uncertainty for the worker in building the client/worker relationship over time.

Thoughts can often have a handicapping impact, with sufferers becoming preoccupied with their delusional content and fearing loss of self-control. Paranoid ideas inevitably create feelings of mistrust and suspicion towards others. The worker must overcome such negative feelings by being constantly reassuring and focusing on the normal and everyday. Cognition can be impaired in terms of poor concentration and understanding. Communication skills are paramount here for the worker. Sentences should be unambiguous in their meaning, concrete, factual and simple, and interviews should be limited to 20 to 30 minutes duration.

Behaviour similarly may be unpredictable and range from overarousal to lethargy. If the client is lethargic, apathetic and lacking in initiative, then the worker must persevere and provide encouragement and motivation. If the client is overaroused, and disinhibited, the worker must remain a calm and still presence, avoiding sudden movements, confrontation or deadlines. The worker can model appropriate social skills, talking in a normal tone of voice, standing at an appropriate distance and engaging in normal eye contact.

Helping family carers

People with enduring mental illnesses often live with their family relatives and, as the MacArthur study revealed, when they behave aggressively it is likely to be in domestic situations with family members. Hostility can result from unwillingness to abide by family rules, jealousy of more functional family members and hypersensitivity to criticism. Research studies have shown that how family relatives communicate with their mentally ill relative is a significant factor in contributing to relapse and hospital readmission. The concept of high emotional expression (high EE) has been identified to describe such an anti-therapeutic style of communication. It is characterised by over-criticism and over-involvement. Families can be taught a more neutral and less antagonistic way of relating which can include components of information-giving, cognitive therapy and stress management (Barrowclough and Tarrier, 2000).

RESEARCH SUMMARY

Violence in the household

Skinner et al.'s study (1992), which involved 1,401 families, found that:

- *20 per cent of relatives with severe mental illness (SMI) had threatened harm;*

- *11 per cent had actually harmed another person;*

- *half the targets were relatives, particularly mothers acting as primary carers.*

CHAPTER SUMMARY

- There are two distinct types of mental disorder associated with a risk of aggression and violence: psychopathic personality disorder and the delusions and hallucinations of schizophrenia and other psychoses.

- It is only when mental illness and substance abuse coexist that there is a higher risk of violence from people with mental illness.

- Aggressive behaviour by people with mental illness occurs more often in domestic home situations and is directed against family members rather than strangers.

- The skills employed when working with clients with mental illness include the use of simple and clear communication, the modelling of appropriate social skills and the use of reassurance and encouragement.

- Families should be calm, non-critical and neutral in their communication with a family member with mental illness.

FURTHER READING

Gould, N (2010) *Mental health social work*. London: Routledge.

This book is an up-to-date, well-informed guide to being a mental health social worker.

Monahan, J, Steadman, HJ, Silver, E, Appelbaum, PS, Clark Robbins, P, Mulvey, EP, Roth, LH, Grisso, T and Banks, S (2001) *Rethinking risk assessment: The MacArthur study of mental disorder and violence*. Oxford: Oxford University Press.

The MacArthur study is the definitive research study of violence and psychiatric hospitalisation.

Stanley, N and Manthorpe, J (2004) *The age of the inquiry: Learning and blaming in health and social care*. London: Routledge.

Although retrospective reasoning about how things might have been done differently has its weaknesses, this book provides an excellent analysis of inquiry findings across the client groups.

Chapter 8

Coping, challenge and conflict in groups

Trevor Lindsay

A C H I E V I N G   A   S O C I A L   W O R K   D E G R E E

This chapter will help you to meet the following National Occupational Standards for Social Work in the UK including the following.
Key Role 2: Plan, carry out, review and evaluate social work practice, with individuals, families, carers, groups, communities and other professionals.
Key Role 6: Demonstrate professional competence in social work practice.

It will also introduce you to the following academic standards as set out in the 2008 social work subject benchmark statement.
5.1.3 Values and ethics.
5.1.4 Social work theory.
5.4 Problem solving skills.
5.6 Communication skills.
5.7 Skills in working with others.

Introduction

In this chapter we will be looking at some challenging situations that may be experienced when working with groups. These can range from resistance where particular members of the group, or the group as a whole, refuse to go along with what the facilitator thinks is best or even what was previously agreed, through disagreement, to hostility and naked aggression. All of these phenomena arise from conflict in groups and we will use this term generically for convenience. The focus of the chapter will be on these situations where they occur when facilitating specially constructed small groups which have been brought together, usually by a social worker, with the aim of intervening in a way that is helpful to the individual, group, organisation or community; in other words, groupwork as a social work method. However, these are not the only group situations in which social workers experience conflict and challenge. This equally can be the case in team meetings, in multi-disciplinary meetings or when we meet a community group or a service users' or carers' action group. This chapter, while not having these situations as a focus, should, nevertheless, prove helpful in dealing with these situations also.

The chapter will start with an attempt to de-pathologise conflict in groups; we need to understand what is happening in these situations from a theoretical rather than emotional perspective. This will lead us into a discussion of the processes that occur in groups and will be followed by some suggestions about how to react in appropriate, constructive and helpful ways. Finally we will look at how co-facilitation and consultancy can help us to develop our practice.

ACTIVITY *8.1*

Think back to a situation where conflict or aggression arose in a group of which you were a member. This could be either a situation you observed or where you were involved either as a perpetrator or recipient of aggression. Make a brief note of what took place, then list first the feelings you experienced and secondly your thoughts.

COMMENT

Dealing with conflict, hostility, aggression and resistance can present a challenge to us not only professionally but also at a personal and emotional level. It is in the nature of groups that things can get out of proportion; emotions can become exaggerated; feelings can be experienced at a deeper level and thinking can become distorted. We will look at some of the reasons for this later in the chapter.

RESEARCH SUMMARY

Williams (1966) identified the most common anxieties experienced by trainee group facilitators. These were:

- *encountering unmanageable resistance;*

- *losing control of the group;*

- *excessive hostility breaking out;*

- *acting out by group members;*

- *overwhelming dependency demands;*

- *group disintegration.*

You will have noted that a theme of anxiety about conflict runs through this list. Anecdotal evidence from students about their groupwork facilitation indicates that the area in which they feel least comfortable is dealing with the unexpected difficulties that occur. By definition, these situations are difficult to be prepared for. This chapter aims to eradicate or reduce some of these anxieties by increasing your understanding of conflict in groups and by equipping you with some strategies to use when it arises.

Reconceptualising conflict

Most people do not enjoy conflict and when it happens in a group it is easy to fall into the trap of seeing it as being caused by the individuals in the group: if only they could be better behaved the problem would not arise. Frequently, conflict in the group as a whole is more usefully understood as a symptom of some other problem related to the group process, the planning or resources of the group, or the conduct of the groupworker/s.

Process in groupwork

An understanding of process is essential for the group facilitator. First we need to understand what we mean by *process* and how it differs from *content*. When we make bread the content of the loaf is the ingredients – flour, yeast, salt, water, etc.; the making of the bread involves a number of processes – mixing the ingredients, rising the dough, applying heat to make the bread; the ingredients are changed in the process so that they become something different – bread. Benson (2009) explains how content refers to the 'what' of group experience – what people are doing and saying, what they are going to do next. Content is the substance of what is happening in the group; it is on the surface and can be seen or heard. Process, on the other hand, happens below the surface. It can rarely be seen or heard but can, nevertheless, be experienced and felt. Process is about the 'how' of individual and group experience – how people react to certain circumstances or are behaving towards each other, how the group acts together. It is reflected in the quality of the group experience. Through the processes that occur in the group, like the bread ingredients, it becomes different. Douglas (2000) explains that all that 'process' means *is that there are discernible patterns of behaviour which tend to emerge in groups over time and appear to focus around certain aspects of the group's behaviour* (p36). The most fundamental process of all, he asserts, is interaction. Douglas (1995) says that the term is used to mean *all the things, which happen in communication between individuals* **... but not the actual words** (p47) (my emphasis). Process concerns what occurs as a result of the words.

CASE STUDY

After a group has been running for some time, one of the members, Monica, says that she is getting bored with the group; the discussion just seems to go round and round in circles. The members of the group react to this statement in different ways. Some of the members ignore it and carry on with their discussion as before. One member of the group, Janice, says she agrees with Monica and has been feeling the same way. Other members feel angry and resentful; they have found the group discussion very helpful and think that Monica and Janice are being very negative. These feelings result in people acting differently; some start to ignore Monica and Janice. Simon on the other hand suddenly discloses a piece of very personal information. This leads to him being attacked by another member.

Here we discern both content and process. What Monica says is part of the content of the group. The consequences of what she has said and in particular, the patterns that arise (for example, Janice always supports her; Simon gets attacked), form part of the process.

ACTIVITY **8.2**

This activity will help you identify 'process' and clarify the differences between content and process issues in situations from your own experience. Select two or three different groups or meetings that you have experienced and see if you can differentiate between the content and processes within each.

- **The content**. *When did people arrive? Who was there? What did they do? What did they say? Was there an agenda? Was it followed? Who interrupted? Who dominated? Who didn't seem to say or do anything? What decisions were made?*

- **The process issues**. *What happened next? How did the group work together? What emotions arose? Where did they come from? How did people react to what was said? Did they react differently to each other? Were there links between what was said, emotional responses and what was said or done next?*

COMMENT

When you think about it, you are dealing with both content and process all the time. Often you realise that what someone has said has more meaning than you first thought, for example when a client asks if you have any children, but you realise that they are asking if you have enough experience to be working with them and their family.

Models of group process

There are a number of models that can help us understand group process. We have space for only two. Benson (2009) uses the polarities of *love* and *will*. He uses *love* to refer to the natural human desire to be attached, to be a part of a larger unit and to take part in a social experience larger than oneself. *Will* is the urge to be individual and separate, to retain one's own identity. All the time in a group, every individual experiences these two competing urges. The love urge manifests itself in things like making friends, joining in, sharing and trusting but it also can result in taking sides and cliquishness and it brings with it distortions like jealousy, suspicion and hostility. The will urge results in behaviour such as people starting things, organising, leading, solving problems and confronting undesirable behaviour. Its counter side brings about such elements as rivalry, stubbornness, selfishness, bullying and aggression. Each individual in the group has to resolve these competing urges in themselves and it is through this resolution that the group finds new behaviours, moves forward and so grows and matures.

Whitaker (2001) uses a similar idea of competing forces to explain group process. Whitaker's group focal conflict theory, in simplified terms, works as follows. Sometimes an impulse emerges in a group. Whitaker calls this a *disturbing motive*. This can be a wish, a desire or a hope. If there is nothing to stand in its way, this shared wish is openly expressed and becomes a theme for discussion. The group, for example, may wish that the discussion becomes more personal and that the members become more self-disclosing. However, a wish is often accompanied by a fear or guilt and this fights against its emergence. In our example, people are frightened that they may be hurt by how others react to their self-disclosure. This is called a *reactive motive*. A conflict, therefore, arises for which the group must find a solution. The group may find a *restrictive solution*, which deals with the fear at the expense of the wish, or an *enabling solution*, which deals with the fear but also allows the expression of the wish. In this way fears are contained and the group is able to explore the associated impulses and emotions. In our example a restrictive solution would be for the group to decide that disclosure is far too risky and a norm therefore arises that members do not disclose personal information, keeping only to safe topics. It is restrictive because it prevents the group from moving forward. An enabling solution might be the recognition that we all have issues that are difficult to disclose but that we can help deal with them when we bring them into the open; it is helpful both for the individual and for others, who may share the problem, for there to be discussion about the issue. A norm arises in the group that people are respected, valued and treated with care when they make a disclosure. In this way, the group moves to a new level of interaction. Whitaker argues that conflict can become established in a group where some of the members press for a particular solution (enabling or restrictive) and others in the group fight against it. She terms this *solutional conflict*. Whitaker uses group focal conflict theory to explain a number of familiar phenomena in groups: the moods or atmospheres that develop such as frivolity or depression, and behaviour which the facilitator may perceive as unhelpful in terms of the group's development but is in fact functional, in some way, for the group. We can see from both these models of process that conflict in a group is not only inevitable but also can be constructive, leading to positive change and development.

Related to ideas about process are theories about how groups change and develop. This is sometimes referred to as stages theory. There are a large number of stages theories, the best known of which is probably Tuckman's (1965) model of 'forming, storming, norming and performing' (for a fuller discussion of stages theory see Benson, 2009; Lindsay and Orton, 2008; Brown, 1994). Common to most of the theories is the idea of conflict as a normal and predictable part of the developing group. Tuckman's storming stage, for example, suggests that, as people begin to feel a little more comfortable and self-assured in the group, members start to seek an individual role and space. There can be jostling for positions of power in the group. Testing out takes place when people make judgements about whether the group is likely to be of value to individuals. As a facilitator you may come under serious attack and need to understand that, while difficult, this is a normal part of group development and does not reflect on you personally. (At the same time, however, there may be very good reasons why you are being challenged, which are nothing to do with 'storming', and do reflect on you personally.)

Douglas (1991) identifies five potentially problematic areas for group facilitators and it will be obvious to you that any one of these can be a cause of conflict in the group.

1. How the facilitator/s perform the role – what they know and how well they know it, their style of facilitation, their level of skill and the roles they adopt in the group, their aims and objectives and the extent to which all of these are congruent with any other facilitators involved.

2. Supervision, training and development of groupworkers. This area is closely related to the first.

3. Group members – their individual characteristics and behaviour.

4. The group as a unit or system (whole-group problems) – problems which arise out of the way the group is structured and those which are to do with the nature and quality of the group's performance and processes.

5. The conditions under which the group operates – external factors such as how it is organised, the venue and time and resources allocated to it, issues to do with colleagues, managers and the community; internal factors including the numbers, the construction of the group and how it is designed.

Learning to deal with conflict is often a matter of experience. It is impossible to give advice on how to deal with every conceivable conflict situation. It is better to give you some general responses that you may apply in a variety of situations. However, for more detailed discussion of particular difficult situations, see Douglas (1991) and Whitaker (2001).

Conflict arising from the group itself and its members

When faced with a conflict situation in the group itself, we need to be able to analyse what is going on, so that we can make an appropriate response.

Problem or opportunity?

As Whitaker (2001) suggests, it is useful to understand what is happening as an opportunity rather than a problem. If a group member launches a verbal attack on another, for example, it may be an opportunity to have a useful discussion about issues such as the relationships in the group as a whole, acceptable ways of confronting, the group rules, or to provide feedback. Similarly, a racist, sexist or homophobic remark provides an opportunity for a discussion around those issues. Everything that happens in a group has a cause; sometimes the cause lies outside the group, sometimes within it. In either situation conflict indicates to us that something requires our attention. See it as a warning or a symptom. Try to work out the cause and then you may be able to find the cure.

Problem for whom?

Conflict in the group seen as a big problem by the groupworker may not necessarily be a problem for anyone else. A useful question to ask yourself is: *For whom is this a problem?* If the answer is *only for the facilitator*, then you know it is something which you are going to have to think about in terms of yourself and either adjust to or live with. If the answer is an individual in the group, you need to decide what action to take to protect them from harm. If it is a whole-group problem, then you will need to think in terms of a whole-group response. If it is a problem for people outside of the group, you will probably need to do some work with neighbours, colleagues or whomever it concerns.

CASE STUDY

A group was running very successfully and had reached a stage where a high level of trust and co-operation existed; people had become open and ready to help each other. The facilitators were very pleased and for the next session planned an activity that they felt would be good in taking this work forward. Shortly after the start of the session, two of the members got into a disagreement about what the group should do next. The discussion became quite heated and all the other members joined in, taking sides. One person suggested putting the matter to the vote but others argued strongly against this, saying that it was better to reach either a compromise or a consensus around one option. By the end of the group nothing had been decided. The facilitators felt that the session had been a waste of time and felt quite angry with the group for wasting time arguing rather than getting on with the programme.

COMMENT

Here we have a situation that may be a problem only for the facilitators. The group is going well and all the people are engaging in discussion and working hard to understand each other and to move forward. If there was a risk of harm to some of the group members it would be the responsibility of the facilitators to take some action to protect them, but otherwise perhaps they should allow the group to find its own way.

Who benefits?

Some conflict situations may be functional in some way, either for the group as a whole or for individuals. You need to think of these situations in terms of group process.

CASE STUDY

A carers' support group is discussing the support available from the local social services office. One member becomes very critical of the service he has received and the others join in. They then start talking about social workers and how they have been let down time and time again, becoming more and more angry as time goes on. The facilitators both feel very uncomfortable, especially as some of the people being discussed are colleagues and friends, and try to defend them. This causes even more anger and it starts to feel as though they themselves are under attack, even though no criticism is made of them personally. Then one of the facilitators remembers that she was unable to attend the last group session because of a domestic problem. She raises this with the group, apologising that she had forgotten to explain her absence at the beginning of the session. This led into a useful discussion of the role and motivation of the facilitators in the group and the anger evaporated.

COMMENT

> *In this example we can see that it was functional for the group to displace the anger they felt towards the facilitator onto the safer target of other social workers outside the group. In group focal conflict terms they were adopting a restrictive solution, alleviating the fear that was associated with tackling the facilitator but preventing the group from addressing the real issue and then moving on.*

Responding to individual and whole-group situations

Brown (1994) provides a useful framework of possible responses to difficult situations that may arise out of individual and whole-group scenarios.

'Do nothing'

It is a good idea to wait a little while before making any intervention, providing no one is being hurt. Let the mud settle. Learn to wait, watch and listen. This way you are more likely to attend to the needs of the group rather than your own. It is easy to panic and do something that will make you feel more comfortable rather than think about the group. It is important to give yourself a little time, firstly to make sure you understand what is happening, secondly to see if the problem will resolve itself or turn out not to be a problem, and thirdly to allow the group members themselves to deal with it. The solutions that members come up with are likely to be much more powerful and enduring than those of the facilitators and allowing them to do so is strengthening and empowering. Of course, if the problem persists it is the responsibility of the facilitator to intervene. There will be situations where for the facilitator to take no action may not be seen as either a neutral or strategic response but to be collusion with what is happening. It would be a dereliction of responsibility, for example, to say or do nothing should a member make a racist, sexist or other unacceptable remark.

Indirect approaches

The worker does not confront the situation directly, or indeed even mention the conflict but finds an indirect way of dealing with the problem. For example, the simple tactic of sitting next to someone can be very effective in providing non-verbal support to someone who is being confronted, without drawing unwanted attention to the individual; it may also be a strategy that makes it easier to control someone given to attacking others.

> **CASE STUDY**
>
> *In a group for young people, one member had great difficulty in finding personal control. Typical behaviour was to be inappropriate, noisy and aggressive, making it hard to make any progress. In the light of prior knowledge of the member's home circumstances and after much discussion, the facilitators concluded that the behaviour arose because of the member's difficulty in trusting anyone in the group. In the following session, they introduced an exercise where the group took turns leading blindfolded members around the building. Here the programme was adapted to include an exercise to help the young person to start building trust in the others.*

Direct approaches

Direct approaches involve making explicit reference to the problem. Brown (1992) gives three categories of direct approaches.

- *Speak directly to the individual at the centre of the problem.* For example, if someone has made a sectarian remark, challenge them directly, perhaps by asking them to substantiate what they have just said or asking why they think they are always at the centre of arguments in the group.

- *Speak directly to the rest of the group.* I am wondering why you all seem to attack Mary, when something goes wrong here or I am wondering why nobody ever comes to John's rescue when people are having a go at him. Sometimes saying 'what is', naming the issue, is a sufficient strategy to resolve a difficulty.

- *Speak to the group as a whole.* I am thinking that we don't seem to be very together tonight. There seems to be a lot of conflict and tension around. Has anyone else noticed that? What do you think is going on just now? Maybe we can talk about this for a while and see if we can find a better way forward.

Of these three strategies, Brown suggests the last is to be preferred, as it does not reinforce possible splits in the group, nor does it locate the difficulty in a particular person or persons.

Make contact outside the group

In this strategy the facilitator sees the individual at the centre, either the perpetrator or victim of aggression, privately, to discuss the problem. Before deciding to make contact with a member outside the group, you will need to consider the following. In seeing this person alone, am I missing an opportunity to facilitate a problem that lies in the group but is manifesting itself through this individual? Even if I am satisfied that this is a difficulty concerning this individual, I need to consider whether it will be beneficial to try to resolve it in the group so that all the members can benefit from the intervention. In seeing this person outside the group, am I perhaps making things worse for the person by pathologising them, or worse for the group by entering into a special relationship with this one individual? Making contact outside the group is really a last-choice strategy.

Consultancy

Facilitating a group either on your own or with a co-worker is a difficult and demanding task. Groupwork is almost by definition more complex than one-to-one work as there are so many more variables and you are engaged with so many more people. Facilitators come under pressure from the group. The feelings aroused in the group and the workers can be very powerful. Being aware and coping with your own feelings, recognising and responding to conflict and emotion in the group, while conducting the group programme and following through the group aims all at once is far from easy. Having one or more co-facilitators is often a great help, but the co-working relationship itself introduces another variable in the group equation. Conflict will inevitably arise between the facilitators as well. It is very difficult for co-facilitators to sort out difficulties in their relationship on their own. Often they will conspire together to not discuss them. For all these reasons it is important for groupworkers to have someone acting as a consultant, with whom they can discuss what is happening in the group (and the co-worker relationship if there is one) and to help them think of ways of sorting out issues. During consultancy sessions, the workers can explore the power relationships between them. Issues such as sectarianism, sexuality, race and gender need to be addressed by co-workers in terms of how they work together, what role models they provide, and how they deal with conscious or unconscious sectarianism, sexism or racism directed towards one or more of them. A consultant is a very useful resource. We think that for the new groupworker it is essential.

Students on placement are fortunate to have built-in consultancy in the form of the practice teacher. However, research (Scally and Lindsay, 1997; Lindsay, 2005) shows that the practice teacher may not have much groupwork expertise. In these circumstances, before embarking on a groupwork project, students should negotiate with their practice teachers to ensure that they have access to regular consultancy from someone who has the necessary experience and knowledge.

Consultancy is not the same as supervision. Supervision usually occurs between the worker and the person who has responsibility for agency accountability for the quality of his/her work – the line manager, the practice teacher. Consultancy is about providing a forum for the open exploration of the issues arising in the group. The same person can conduct the two roles, but there may be situations where it is inappropriate for the practice teacher or line manager to undertake this role. We have discussed above the situation where the supervisor does not have enough experience in this area of work. Alternatively, it may be that there are issues to do with the formal or informal power relationships between the co-workers and the supervisor; there may be issues of seniority or inter-agency relationships; the balance in terms of gender or ethnicity may be inappropriate for the group in mind.

Consultation in general, and groupwork consultation in particular, are important subjects in their own right and we have space only to flag up a few basic points.

- Choose the consultant carefully to ensure a productive working relationship.

- Draw up a consultation agreement or contract.

- Arrange for consultation to start from the group planning stage.

- Plan in and diary consultation sessions, just like the other groupwork sessions, to ensure they happen, and do not collude to avoid them when things are rocky.

- Make sure that all understand the focus and agenda of consultation sessions.

- The consultant should adopt a proactive approach in consultation sessions.

- Everyone involved is equally responsible for the success of the consultancy arrangement.

CHAPTER SUMMARY

Facilitating groups can be worrying. Groupwork involves working with a high degree of complexity and unpredictability. Things rarely go exactly to plan and you will need to be prepared to deal with some unexpected situations, including outbursts of aggression, hostility and conflict. It is useful to realise that this is a normal part of groupwork facilitation and not a disaster. Good planning is at the foundation of groupwork practice and will carry you a long way. People will usually forgive you your mistakes when they see that you have been working hard to get it right. Nevertheless, you need to prepare yourself for the unexpected. One way is to realise what is likely to go wrong. Another is to be able to analyse what is happening. You will also need to have a repertoire of responses that you can apply to most situations.

In this chapter, we set out to equip you with some of this knowledge and you should now be aware of the different ways in which difficulties can manifest themselves, some ways in which you can conceptualise these situations and some responses that you can make.

Having someone who is not directly involved in the group can be a great help in untangling issues, either in relation to what is happening in the group, between the facilitators or between the group and the outside.

Confidence in oneself is probably the greatest asset in dealing with difficult situations. Knowledge of yourself combined with optimism and self-belief will help to see you through.

FURTHER READING

Douglas, T (1991) *A handbook of common groupwork problems*. London: Tavistock/Routledge.

This text is entirely devoted to identifying and resolving difficult issues that may arise in groups.

Whitaker, DS (2001) *Using groups to help people*. 2nd edition. Hove: Brunner-Routledge.

This contains the author's focal group conflict theory and also has a useful chapter entitled 'Problems and opportunities', in which she identifies and categorises group situations which you may consider problematic. The author analyses these and provides helpful and straightforward advice on how to deal with them.

Doel, M and Sawdon, C (1999) *The essential groupworker*. London: Jessica Kingsley.

In this you will find descriptions and analysis of eight behaviours that groupworkers can find challenging.

Brown, A (1994) *Groupwork*. 3rd edition. Aldershot: Ashgate Publishing.

Brown identifies similar behaviours and provides a number of possible responses, categorised as described in the text above.

Lindsay, T and Orton, S (2011) *Groupwork practice in social work*. 2nd edition, Exeter: Learning Matters.

The authors include chapters on group process and on coping with difficult situations in groups.

Benson, J (2009) *Working more creatively with groups*. 3rd edition. Abingdon: Routledge.

This contains one of the best accounts of group process.

Chapter 9

Managing conflict in maintaining standards in social care service provision

Mary McColgan and Geraldine Fleming

A C H I E V I N G   A   S O C I A L   W O R K   D E G R E E

This chapter will help you to meet the following National Occupational Standards for Social Work in the UK including the following.
Key Role 1: Prepare for, and work with individuals, families, carers, groups and communities to assess their needs and circumstances.
Key Role 2: Plan, carry out, review and evaluate social work practice, with individuals, families, carers, groups, communities and other professionals.
Key Role 4: Manage risk to individuals, families, carers, groups, communities, self and colleagues.
Key Role 6: Demonstrate professional competence in social work practice.

It will also introduce you to the following academic standards as set out in the 2008 social work subject benchmark statement.
5.1.2 The service delivery context.
5.1.4 Social work theory.
5.1.5 The nature of social work practice.
5.5.4 Intervention and evaluation.
5.6 Communication skills.
5.8 Skills in personal and professional development.

Introduction

This chapter will outline reasons why resistance may be experienced in maintaining quality standards in social care services, how this resistance may be exhibited and what can be done to overcome this. Examples will be drawn from practice with older people, vulnerable adults and early years settings to illustrate the range of issues which may occur for the social work practitioner in a care management role, and to relate good practice guidance in a range of service user groups. Social workers will be reminded about their role in safeguarding vulnerable adults and children, the importance of observation, accurate and timely recording, communication skills, ways of promoting quality standards, and strategies for conveying their professional concerns verbally and in written formats.

We begin by discussing what quality standards are and why they are important, and what the social work role is in maintaining social care standards.

What are quality standards?

Several writers emphasise that quality standards provide a clear indication of how a service will be delivered and significantly define good standards for practice. They also attempt to outline what service users can expect from services and they are linked to social care governance, which is defined as *managerial and clinical leadership and account-ability ... and systems and working practices to enable probity, quality assurance, quality improvement, and patient safety to be the central components of all routines, processes and activities* (McSherry and Warr, 2008, p86).

Why are quality standards important?

There are several reasons why quality standards are important.

1. They provide an understanding of what constitutes good practice and good care for a range of services.

2. They provide a public benchmark for these services and are used by regulatory bodies in determining whether services are appropriate to meet the needs of service users and carers.

3. They also provide national frameworks so consistency is recognised.

4. As the standards are measurable, judgements can be made about the extent to which they are met, so safeguards are in place.

ACTIVITY 9.1

What elements are involved in quality standards?

What is the social work role in ensuring quality standards in social care services?

What elements are included in typical quality standards?

What principles should underpin work in this role?

What activities might be involved in this work?

What challenges might there be?

COMMENT

You might think the elements in Figure 9.1 below are relevant because they suggest that there are core aspects to be found in examining services, and standards are often developed to reflect these. Can you think of other aspects that would be relevant? You might want to add effectiveness and continuous improvement as well as empowering service users to have a voice and participate in decisions affecting their lives.

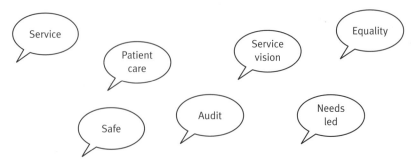

Figure 9.1 Key dimensions of standards in services

CASE STUDY

Older people

Charlie Baird is an 80-year-old man who has dementia. His only close family member is a niece Mary, who is also the controller of his affairs. Mary had been Charlie's main carer until his admission to hospital about 24 months previously. To offer full-time care Mary (and her husband Jim) had moved near to Charlie's home and although she worked part-time Mary had managed to support Charlie to stay in his own home. The admission to hospital had occurred when Charlie fell in the kitchen and sustained a fractured femur.

Prior to his admission to hospital Charlie had requested to move to a private nursing home near to his home. His name was subsequently placed on their waiting list. A place had recently become available and was offered to Charlie. When Mary was informed of the offer, she forcefully stated that she did not wish her uncle to go into private nursing care. Mary argued that in her opinion Charlie would not receive the same standard of care and she had concerns about the practices in the home of sedating older people who experienced dementia because she had worked there briefly before she got her job in a care home; therefore, she would reject the offer on his behalf.

Under the Health Authority policy, if a patient receives an offer of a place in a home of their choice the offer must be accepted. The Health Authority may go ahead and discharge the patient even if the family disagree. The social worker was required to inform Mary of this fact. This led to Mary and her husband telephoning the social worker four or five times each day arguing that the decision was wrong. Each telephone call lasted over 25 minutes with the social worker constantly defending the proposed move. On a number of occasions the telephone conversations became almost adversarial in content.

What might a social worker have to consider when dealing with this case?

A major dilemma for the social worker was trying to fulfil different roles at the same time. The social worker was an employee of the trust, an advocate for Charlie, and also support for his niece Mary. The Health Authority wanted to free up a bed, Mary wanted to keep things as they were, and Charlie was not able to communicate his needs.

As the telephone calls became more adversarial the social worker was in danger of losing sight of their role in the situation. This was to represent Charlie and also his niece, and try to meet their needs within the framework of local authority policy, guidelines and legislation. Details of relevant legislation and policy can be found at the end of the chapter.

Multiple service user systems

In cases of dementia there are almost always multiple service users. Monahan (1993) recommends an ecological-family-centred approach to interventions with dementia service users, placing them within their own context of family, agency, residential institution, and society, taking into account the impact of all of these different systems on the service user.

The majority of the social worker's interaction was not with Charlie, but with his niece and hospital staff. All of the rapport and interpersonal relationship is built up with the family and carers, not the person suffering from dementia. There is always a danger that the social worker will forget who the main service user is and prioritise the rights and wishes of the carer/family members above the dementia sufferer.

The welfare of Charlie was of paramount importance in this situation. His consultant had assessed him as medically fit for discharge to the private nursing home. However, Mary's anxieties about his care in the nursing home have led to a situation where she is reluctant to consider this as a viable option for him and consequently she has refused to accept the offer on his behalf. There are ethical issues to consider also because Charlie is not able to make an informed decision about his care and the issue of mental capacity is relevant.

Mental capacity

The Mental Capacity Act 2005 in England and Wales provides legal protection for vulnerable individuals who lack capacity by setting out key principles and safeguards. The Human Rights Act links into the Mental Capacity Act. A social worker must assume that everyone can make a decision unless proved otherwise. An individual can make a decision if:

- they understand the information given;
- they can retain and weigh up this information;
- they are able to communicate their decision (verbally/written/body language/sign language/pictorially).

Effective communication

Professional social work activity is guided by professional codes of conduct and each devolved region has developed codes to underpin social work practice. Social workers are responsible for making sure that their conduct does not fall below the standards set out in the code. In Northern Ireland, the Northern Ireland Social Care Council (NISCC) has set criteria for employers and staff including social workers. In the context of the case study possible standards may include: *Standard 2: Strive to establish and maintain the trust and confidence of service user and carers*. This is of particular significance when considering effective communication because:

- it is important that social care workers adapt their communication style to suit the service user and recognise that all behaviour is a form of communication;

- the social worker's communication style can influence the service user's ability to communicate effectively.

Research has shown that 7 per cent of meaning is in the words that are spoken, with 38 per cent of meaning in the way that the words are said. For example, when a social worker puts more stress on certain words, uses pauses between words to convey seriousness or interest; or varies the tone and speed of utterances, the importance of certain words or phrases are underlined in the mind of the service user. In addition, cultural issues may affect how the individual communicates. For example, Mary may not have been encouraged within her culture to express her anger in a less aggressive manner.

Tone of voice and pace of delivery are very important when holding a telephone conversation, as is actively listening to not only the spoken responses, but also the silences. Active listening skills involve resisting the temptation to interrupt and also avoiding jumping to conclusions. In addition, if you become anxious and even angry, this can easily be interpreted as being disrespectful by not listening. By not being able to read the parties' non-verbal cues, the social worker felt angry, thereby allowing the situation to escalate with both parties becoming defensive regarding their respective situations.

For controlled emotion, you need to develop awareness of early recognition of the triggers which can lead to physiological changes in the body resulting in an unhelpful or inappropriate response. Employing cognitive behavioural techniques such as deep breathing, counting to five, etc., can assist you in employing more measured and less adversarial approaches when dealing with outpourings of anger and aggression. The concept of working with resistance lies at the heart of the case study and in the following section we consider why this is important and how resistance can be addressed.

Understanding and managing resistance

Resistance constitutes a form of power and control within a given situation. The resistance could come from relatives who find it difficult to accept certain options, or an older person refusing to recognise the risks inherent in their failing mobility, or an organisation failing to meet minimum quality standards for the provision of care. Their resistance to engaging with you is a demonstration of their position and perspective.

Resistance is a multi-layered phenomenon that takes diverse and complex forms. While it is undeniable that resistance can have positive aspects, it typically conjures up ideas of stubbornness, defiance, inflexibility, opposition and intractability. It is not helpful to consider it in these terms and within this section we will look more closely at resistance and identify ways to understand why there is resistance and how to work with it. Theories of resistance are useful tools for understanding and intervening in situations you may encounter within your social work role. There is a duality inherent in the roles and responsibilities of social work. Legal and ethical mandates frame the working relationship and undoubtedly contribute to resistance to change. A clear understanding of resistance to engagement can, to a large degree, influence how you work with and manage resistance.

Table 9.1 Reasons for resistance

Organisational	Interpersonal
• defence against the stress of implementing a change	• defence against the stress of implementing a change
• denial of the impact of not changing	• denial of the need/drivers for change
• concern about potential cost of change	• concern about the impact of engaging
• lacks the knowledge or ability to engage and implement change	• lacks the knowledge or ability to engage and implement change
• lacks understanding of the mandate to change	• lacks understanding of the mandate for change
• being influenced by external factors	• being influenced by external factors
• perceptions of previous experience vulnerable adult	• perceptions of previous experiences as a vulnerable adult

Lewin's force field analysis

Resistance to change is well researched and analysed within the field of organisational management. There are various tools available to support analysis of resistance. Working with individual resistance presents with many of the same features as organisational resistance. In the first instance when resistance is encountered it is essential to examine and understand the present situation and plan the steps you need to take to address the causes of the resistance. Lewin's force field is a useful tool; it assumes that in any change situation there are two sets of forces. These are the forces seeking to drive change and those resisting change (Martin and Henderson, 2001).

Within social care and the client/practitioner relationship this proves a useful tool in analysing and planning necessary work and delivering beneficial outcomes. So this understanding of how resistance occurs can help to influence practice. In the next example, we consider what responses are required when concerns arise in a children's day care setting.

CASE STUDY

Early years

Mary has felt annoyed by the hospital's refusal to keep her uncle in hospital while she negotiates alternative arrangements. She contemplates taking him home to live with Jim and her children but realises that she would have to bring his bed downstairs and they do not have the room to accommodate this. To add to her stress, she has concerns about Frank's behaviour. He has been attending a local nursery and she was relieved to get a place there for him three mornings a week. Although he was unsettled at the beginning, he has been happy to go there until three weeks ago when he had an accident

Continued

at the nursery and came home with another set of clothes. When she asked him what had happened, he just said he had been a bad boy and although she had comforted him, Frank seemed reluctant to talk about it. She queried the situation with the nursery leader and learned that a new worker had started in the nursery. The new worker was the mother of one of her colleagues in the care home. She was in her 50s and was a grandmother herself. Mary had been happy to see her in the nursery and felt she had experience of caring for her own children and would bring a common-sense approach to her work. However, when Mary gets a chance to talk to her about Frank, the worker's response alarms her. She states that children of Frank's age should be toilet trained and her child-rearing practices have taught her that firm discipline is what is required. Mary is horrified to hear such views expressed and realises that she must challenge the worker's attitudes and values. She is worried about the standards of the nursery if such behaviour is allowed to continue and wonders how she will deal with the situation. What advice would you give Mary?

At the outset, it is important to consider the issue of quality standards in early years settings (Lindon, 2008; Pugh, 1996). Moss and Pence (1994), having examined theories on quality, concluded that quality was a very subjective concept based on values, beliefs and interests and that the approach to defining quality in early childhood services had been exclusionary in nature, and has involved the exercise of power and control. They put forward an inclusionary paradigm for defining quality based on participation from and sharing of the beliefs, values and interests of a broad range of stakeholders. Laevres (1994) defined three core elements of quality as providing opportunities for independence, being tuned to a child's needs and feelings, and the nature of the interactions and interventions with children.

The Effective Provision of Pre-School Education (EPPE) 2004 was the first European study of child development between the ages of three and seven years. The study found that pre-school provision enhanced the educational prospects of children and contributed to the intellectual development of the under-threes. High-quality pre-school provision was associated with improvements in children's social behaviour. Similar benefits were found when caregivers in pre-school settings were responsive to children's needs (Smith, 1999).

The Effective Pre-School Provision in Northern Ireland study 2006 established that high-quality pre-school provision offers children an advantage in terms of their social, emotional and cognitive development which has a long-lasting effect. The study contended that quality was a subjective term, dependent on different variables and perspectives, so reducing quality to checklists was difficult. Research from the USA suggests that quality is closely linked to qualified staffing levels, low turnover and effective leadership. In essence, a qualified workforce formed the basis of quality standards because staff understand children's needs and can respond appropriately.

Continued

RESEARCH SUMMARY *continued*

Research conducted across Northern Ireland and the Republic of Ireland (McColgan et al., 2006) found that parents were concerned about a number of factors in childcare provision. The research was based on a participatory action research approach which combined a community-based survey of parents and focus groups. The survey was conducted by women from community network organisations who were trained to administer questionnaires within their local areas. A total of 966 questionnaires were returned (a 63.5 per cent return rate), providing the perspectives of a very diverse range of parents and producing data in relation to 1,909 children. Parents were primarily concerned about trust and reliability of services. They felt that the availability of vetted staff and the good reputation of the provider were the key factors in influencing parental choice of childcare. These factors were rated more highly than issues of cost and location but the safety of children was their prime concern.

If Mary raised her concerns with social services, they would normally instigate an investigation. However, Mary may choose to raise her concerns with the manager of the nursery and before doing so, she needs to be aware that in accordance with regulations, the nursery will have clear procedures and processes for dealing with allegations about staff. Mary needs to collate her information, providing factual details about what Frank said, how he talked about the incident and what she observed about his behaviour. In her discussions with the manager, she must not adopt a tone of voice which could be regarded as accusatory and she should explain her concerns for Frank's well-being while at the nursery. The concerns may be regarded as evidence of poor practice and the allegations could form part of a disciplinary investigation. In any case, proper procedures would have to be followed and these could lead to dismissal and referral to the fitness for practice procedures of the regulatory body.

ACTIVITY 9.2

Consider the following recording of concerns.

What Frank said: *On Tuesday 2 November at 4 p.m., when Mary was driving Frank home from nursery, he asked Mary when would he be a 'big boy' because Mrs Smyth told him big boys do not wear nappies.*

How he talked about the incident: *He seemed worried about this and was crying.*

What behaviour was observed: *He wanted Mary to stay with him in the nursery and take him to the toilet. He had cried a lot recently when he had had 'accidents'.*

Mrs Smyth's response: *Mary spoke to Mrs Smyth the next day, 3 November at 8.30 a.m. when she left Frank off at the nursery. Mrs M said, He should be toilet trained by now and you just need to be firm with him. I have reared three grandchildren and they were toilet trained long before your son. Without waiting for a response from Mary, Mrs Smyth talked about how she had used a 'star chart' to good effect and suggested that Mary needed to be firm with Frank so he did not get his own way.*

Mary felt annoyed about several things; what might these be?

> **COMMENT**
>
> *There are several aspects which might cause Mary to feel distressed. She may feel she is facing accusations about her parenting skills or Mrs Smyth is insinuating she was an expert in rearing children because she is a grandparent. Mary may be concerned about Mrs Smyth's lack of understanding about children's development or the possible stereotyping towards Frank and the poor value base which did not respect children's uniqueness. She may be worried about the potential emotional abuse of the comments to Frank, the abuse of a trusting relationship between an adult carer and a child as well as the inappropriate way in which concerns were raised and the patronising attitude conveyed by Mrs Smyth towards Mary herself. This demonstrates possible failure to work in partnership with Mary and recognise her expertise as a parent. You may feel that it was inappropriate for Mrs Smyth to make comparisons between Mary's child and the grandchildren, suggesting that Frank's behaviour was not consistent with developmental milestones. Moreover, you might highlight the possible failure to comply with agency policy and procedures in safeguarding children.*

In addressing these concerns there are a number of areas for consideration, including:

- the quality of Mrs Smyth's one-to-one care of Frank, her qualifications and training for the role in the nursery;

- her attitudes and values as conveyed through her behaviour and her comments;

- her understanding of children's development.

However, the line manager also has responsibility for her performance as an employee in the nursery and the service itself is subject to ongoing inspections by the appropriate government department so there are implications for meeting quality standards requirements.

The following section outlines steps which could be instigated by the agency in investigating Mary's concerns.

Stages involved in dealing with an allegation or suspicion of abuse

Recording concerns

As your records may be subject to some level of review, judicial or otherwise, accurate and timely record-keeping is essential. Record-keeping will include accurate details of the referral to both social services and the police and you will need to ensure that you complete the appropriate forms and record the date and time of any information shared. In addition, you will need to outline any communication between key agencies, providing details of core information. Details about strategy meetings and case conferences will need to contain explicit information about what reports were shared, what facts they contained and how the decisions were made. It is important to record the basis for the decision, the agreement of the parties concerned and note any dissenting views. Normally, agreed actions are outlined and timescales identified. If appropriate, details of witness statements and medical examinations should be included. It is important not to convey any opinions unless they are based on facts you have either witnessed or can substantiate yourself, otherwise this information will be regarded as hearsay evidence.

Template for report recording concerns

This could involve a number of aspects. You would need to record details of the initial cause for concern with date and time, noting who had brought the matter to your attention. Then you should have a factual record of what happened and indicate whether there were any previous incidents, how these had been dealt with and noting any outcomes. It is important to provide a picture of the vulnerable adult with a social history of their circumstances, social and family networks including an assessment of their capacity to consent and understanding of the present situation. You need to provide information about the alleged abuse and the person alleged to be responsible, detailing the location of the cause of abuse (where it took place) and its nature (what form it is alleged to have taken and who may have witnessed it). Bearing in mind that your report may form the basis of further action, you should include a description of the investigation process, what was involved and the level of co-operation received from the various people involved. Another important aspect involves your evaluation of the evidence and your assessment of the seriousness of the alleged abuse. You will need to highlight any risks and base your recommendations on clear opinions and conclusions of the evidence base.

CASE STUDY

Physical disability

Joanna Campbell has recently moved into a small flat beside Mary's uncle. She is 56 years old with chronic liver disease and a history of alcohol misuse. Joanna was discharged from hospital six months ago with a domiciliary care package to meet her personal care needs. Joanna has little or no contact with family and no informal support networks. Her social worker, Garry, is newly qualified. He has been trying to contact Joanna, by letter and phone, to arrange a home visit to review the care package but has had no response from Joanna. Garry visits Joanna at her flat and finds her in an unkempt state. There is evidence that Joanna may be drinking again (beer cans around the room) and her health has further deteriorated. Joanna presents as lethargic, listless and jaundiced though there is no evidence she has been drinking today. Joanna agrees Garry can contact her GP and request an urgent home visit. Garry rings the surgery and this is arranged. Garry explores with Joanna the events since he last saw her.

Joanna tells Garry everything is going well but sometimes the carers do not arrive. She is not clear when this has happened but tells him things worked well until recently. She also tells Garry some old friends have been visiting her and she is happy to have the company as she has felt lonely since leaving hospital though she admits they bring alcohol with them and she had been drinking. He highlights the deterioration he sees and Joanna acknowledges the reappearance of her old friends, her resumption of drinking and the current deterioration are all linked. Garry reminds her that she was re-housed to a different area to try to help her break old patterns of behaviour.

Continued

> **CASE STUDY** *continued*
>
> *On examining the domiciliary provider's home record, Garry sees that several visits have not taken place in the past six weeks with no explanation recorded and other visits have been abandoned with comments client refused service and client has taken drink. Garry recognises the situation is complex with many interrelated factors. The GP visits and after some time with Joanna informs Garry that he is arranging for Joanna to go into hospital as he is concerned about her liver function. As the doctor leaves, the care worker arrives for a scheduled visit. Garry and Joanna update her on the hospital admission and the care worker helps Joanna pack some things she will need in hospital. The care worker tells Garry she has been concerned about Joanna and has told her supervisor. Garry decides with Joanna's admission to hospital his immediate concerns about her safety are not an imminent concern but one he must pursue. On returning to the office he speaks to his line manager to agree the next steps he should take.*

> **COMMENT**
>
> *Consider how Garry should respond, considering:*
>
> - *Joanna's rights, needs and risks;*
>
> - *policies for safeguarding vulnerable adults;*
>
> - *communication and dealing with resistance;*
>
> - *social care governance including duties of care and quality;*
>
> - *use of supervision and managing risk.*

Using supervision

The function of supervision is defined throughout a wide range of writings on the subject as consisting of a number of elements that can be categorised under three broad themes: administration, education and support (Hawkins and Shohet, 1989; Morrison, 2001). Professional supervision can be formal, a regularly scheduled, minuted meeting, either one-to-one or group sessions with an agreed contract between the professional supervisor and supervisee. Supervision can also take place on an informal or *ad hoc* basis dealing with issues and concerns as they occur. *Ad hoc* supervision often deals with practice issues, crisis response and safeguarding concerns. Good professional supervision is a process that underpins critical reflection, continuous professional development and learning. It ensures good governance and accountability, addresses outcomes for clients, supports social workers with complex work and decision-making and supports service development. In the case study that we are considering, Garry outlines the situation to his manager, Colm. It is agreed that the first priority is to ensure Joanna's safety – as Joanna is now in hospital, Colm agrees this is met. However, he is clear that Joanna's home situation requires consideration under the Safeguarding Protocol and Colm makes the referral to the safeguarding designated officer to begin the process.

Safeguarding concerns

The safeguarding of vulnerable adults is a paramount concern in social work practice. Recent developments in research, social policy, legislation, demographic changes, societal context and attitudes inform and shape care practices in safeguarding work. The various types of abuse identified by the Department of Health (DoH, 2000) are:

- physical abuse;

- sexual abuse;

- psychological abuse;

- financial or material abuse;

- neglect or acts of omission;

- institutional abuse;

- discriminatory abuse.

ACTIVITY **9.3**

What do you think has informed the decision to consider Joanna to be a vulnerable adult?

What do you think the potential areas of abuse are in Joanna's situation with reference to the list above?

COMMENT

Garry discusses with Colm the care provider issues reported by Joanna, the home record and his brief conversation with the care worker while they helped Joanna prepare for her hospital admission. Garry emphasises his concern that he was not made aware of the changes in Joanna's situation by the care provider. Colm discusses the provider's responsibility to report changes in circumstances, concerns and failure to deliver services and Garry agrees to contact the care provider to inform them of Joanna's hospital admission and discuss the issues he has identified. They also discuss how Garry will be open in his communication and use active listening skills to gather information from the care provider on recent events. Colm asks Garry to keep him informed of progress with the care provider. Garry is aware Colm has a clear social care governance responsibility in this situation, as have the line manager and designated officer within safeguarding protocols.

In tuning in to the situation with the service provider there are a number of aspects that Garry considers.

- The difficulties providers can encounter, especially when working in situations where alcohol or drugs are involved.

- The advocacy role inherent in social work.

- The identified needs of the client not being met.

- The potential risks for clients when there are problems with service delivery.

- The need to ask open questions to engage the provider and hear the provider's views.

- The duty to represent the organisation's governance and accountability responsibilities, ensuring good standards of care are maintained.

- Garry recognises his own dissatisfaction with the care provider's actions and considers Joanna's situation was exacerbated by their failure to keep him informed of the situation.

- The need to maintain a clear record of this discussion.

- The possibility that the care provider will be resistant or ambivalent to the issues identified.

RESEARCH SUMMARY

In the early 1990s a major reform of social welfare services for adults was implemented in Great Britain and Northern Ireland. This included the creation of home care (as opposed to the existing 'home help') services to support older people in their own homes as a preferred alternative to residential and nursing home care. However, the introduction of this service is not without issues, not least because of the interplay between risks to the client and risks to the home care worker which need to be considered in decisions about providing such services.

This grounded theory study gathered interview and focus group data from 99 professionals in statutory health and social care services across Northern Ireland. This included social workers (in both hospitals and in the community), home care service managers, consultant geriatricians, general medical practitioners, nurses and allied health professionals. The aim was to explore their judgements and decisions about long-term care for older people including risk in home care services.

The study illustrated the many and diverse hazards faced by home care workers as they visited older people at all hours and in all seasons, ranging across hygiene and infection, manual handling, aggression and harassment, domestic and farm animals, fleas and sometimes questionable safety of home equipment.

The study highlighted the conflict that can sometimes arise between the right of the older person to choice and dignity and the right of the home care worker to a healthy and safe environment for work. As the client's own home might be considered as the place of work for the home care worker, decisions about home care services need to take into account the responsibilities of the employer to ensure safe working conditions for their employee. Something accepted unquestioningly as a normal hazard of life by the client, perhaps over decades, may be unacceptable to the home care worker or to the employing organisation. There may be a conflict between the rights of the client under human rights legislation and the duties of the employer under health and safety legislation in areas such as the use of hoists for lifting as opposed to manual lifting by home care workers. A particularly difficult decision is the point at which a service might be withdrawn because of the risk to the home care worker (Taylor and Donnelly, 2006).

Garry speaks to one of the supervisors he knows through other clients he works with. Anne, the home care services supervisor, tells Garry she is glad he has contacted her about Joanna as things have been difficult and they are on the verge of withdrawing the service.

On further discussion Garry identifies the following.

• The provider notes the care package was working well up until about eight weeks ago when Joanna began drinking.

• The care workers report that often there are other 'drinking buddies' at the flat while they are trying to deliver the service.

• The care workers often feel vulnerable and 'outnumbered' in this situation.

• Joanna has been verbally aggressive to the carers and on a couple of occasions ordered them from the flat.

• Joanna has refused care on numerous occasions.

• The carers have reported that when preparing breakfast for Joanna there is no food in the house.

• Anne does not accept that all this information should have been passed to Garry immediately.

• Garry reminds Anne of their duty to care, the care standards and the contract arrangements.

• Anne explains to Garry she has a duty of care towards her staff and that their employer has duties under health and safety legislation and requirements to provide safe conditions of work.

• Anne considers that as the provider they were working to 'turn around the situation'.

• Finally, Anne notes that if Joanna's behaviour and the situation do not improve, they will withdraw the service and advises Garry she plans to speak with her manager and he should consider other arrangements for Joanna when she is due to be discharged from hospital.

Anne seems unprepared to accept Garry's points that the care provider has a responsibility to inform him of all changes and that failure to pass on information may have contributed to the deterioration in Joanna's health.

ACTIVITY **9.4**

Addressing resistance

Review the information Garry has gathered in relation to the provider's approach and Joanna's situation.

Why do you think there is such resistance in this case and how should Garry plan to work with this situation?

COMMENT

Garry records the details of the discussion with Anne clearly and accurately. He speaks with Colm again, updating him on the resistance he has encountered in talking to the provider and his additional concerns. Colm also updates Garry and confirms he has had a discussion with the hospital social work manager and the strategy discussion under safeguarding procedures has been scheduled. They agree Garry will prepare a detailed report to inform the safeguarding investigation. Garry now needs to inform the care provider that an investigation under safeguarding procedure is underway and that the designated officer will be informing the relevant regulatory authority.

Garry speaks initially to Anne and informs her of how matters in regards to Joanna's situation and the provider's involvement will proceed. Anne explains to Garry she has had a discussion with her own manager. Garry notes a marked change in Anne's attitude and she highlights the organisation's commitment to the safeguarding investigation. She also explains her manager's plan to instigate an internal investigation.

ACTIVITY 9.5

Review the various aspects of this case and how Garry has identified the relevant issues. In particular, consider how he dealt with the safeguarding and governance aspects and how he used supervision to support his understanding and actions.

CHAPTER SUMMARY

This chapter has considered the reasons why resistance can be experienced when conflict emerges in maintaining standards in social care provision. Through three case studies, the chapter has explained what standards are, why they are important and how resistance might be expressed. In defining the social work role the chapter also considered what verbal and non-verbal skills would be effective in managing conflict. We have highlighted various ways in which resistance may be manifested through individual behaviour or organisational responses and explored how professional practice needs to be underpinned by such aspects as recording, supervision and social care governance.

FURTHER READING

Department of Health (2003) *Domiciliary care: National minimum standards: Regulations.* London: DoH (England and Wales) **www.dh.gov.uk**

Department of Health, Social Services and Public Safety (2003) *Domiciliary care agencies: Minimum standards.* Belfast: DHSSPS (Northern Ireland) **www.dhsspsni.gov.uk/domiciliary_care_ standards**

These documents set out national minimum standards for domiciliary care agencies including statutory provision. The purpose of these minimum standards is to ensure the quality of personal care and support which people receive while living in their own home in the community. These documents identify a standard of service provision below which an agency providing personal care for people living in their own home must not fall. While broad in scope, these standards acknowledge the unique and complex needs of individuals, and the additional specific knowledge and skills required in order to deliver a service that is tailored to the needs of each person. These standards are applicable to personal care for a wide range of people who need care and support while living in their own home.

Department for Children, Schools and Families, Department of Health, Department for Work and Pensions (2008) *Raising standards – Improving outcomes: Statutory guidance: Early years Outcomes Duty: Childcare Act 2006.* London: DCSF.

This guidance provides an overview of the duties that are key to how local authorities and their partners work together to promote early childhood services and improve outcomes including consideration of structures, accountabilities, processes and performance management systems.

Hawkins, P and Shohet, R (1989) *Supervision in the helping professions: An individual, group and organizational approach.* Milton Keynes: Open University Press.

Although written for the supervisor rather than the supervisee, this gem of a book will be valuable reading for supervisees also. It includes a chapter devoted to supervisees getting the most out of supervision as well as addressing a variety of issues and contexts such as stress and burnout. It is comprehensive and also readable.

Simmons, L (2007) *Social care governance: A practice workbook.* Belfast: Department of Health, Social Services and Public Safety (Clinical and Social Care Governance Support Team) and London: Social Care Institute for Excellence.

Somerset County Council and SCIE (2011) *Social care governance: A workbook based on practice in England: Workforce development SCIE guide 38.* London: Social Care Institute for Excellence.

These documents, published in the usual very readable SCIE style, focus on achieving quality in social care services, which is a combination of individual, team and organisational responsibility. Organising our efforts to achieve quality effectively is the purpose of social care governance. This is achieved by teams reflecting in a structured way on the service they currently provide and then on how it could be developed. Social care governance is a framework for ensuring that social care services provide high ethical standards of service and continue to improve them. Our values, behaviours, decisions and processes are open to scrutiny as we develop safe and effective evidence-based practice. Good governance means that we recognise our accountability, we act on lessons learned and we are honest and open in seeking the best possible outcomes and results for people.

Conclusion

Brian J Taylor

This book has been written primarily to address the need among students on qualifying social work professional training to develop the knowledge and skills to work with clients and families who are less than enthusiastic about the help and support offered, and those who may be aggressive. Numerically the majority of social work clients are grateful for the help and support given, particularly at times of crisis and life-changing decisions about care. However, social work frequently involves working with more reluctant clients, such as where children or adults must be protected from abuse or offenders are being supervised. Sometimes the pressures to engage with a social worker experienced by the client are from other family members such as in some mental health, marital counselling and addiction work.

Theoretical sources

The earlier chapters in this book have laid a foundation for later chapters by considering definitions of terms (Chapter 1), theories of aggression (Chapter 2) and general principles for avoiding assault and defusing aggressive situations (Chapter 3). We have considered passive and active expressions of anger, and how ambivalence can arise if clients want help but also have emotions pulling in a different direction. We have considered theories of aggression in terms of theories related to human biology, growth, development and instinct; theories related to how humans respond to stimuli and experience; and theories related to how we think and learn, and function within family, group and social systems.

In addressing the issues discussed in this book, remember to build on the fundamental social work knowledge and skills, both interpersonal (Shulman, 2009) and in managing care (Taylor and Devine, 1993). Clarifying your role is absolutely essential and may require more work in a situation of conflict to avoid misunderstanding. You need to make it clear what is negotiable and what is not. Practice should model social work values, such as seeking collaborative problem-solving within the constraints of what is possible. The traditional skills of reflective listening and empathy should not be underestimated in their value in engaging a resistant client and building as productive a working relationship as is possible in the circumstances. Belief in the client's capacity to engage and to change is fundamental to human helping processes. Increasingly research evidence points to the value of focused approaches such as task-centred casework (McColgan, 2009), motivational interviewing (Miller and Rollnick, 2002) solution-focused brief therapy (Lindsay I, 2009) and other brief therapies (Abbass et al., 2006) with resistant as well as more co-operative clients.

Resistant clients

As discussed in the chapters of this book, sometimes clients can be resistant because the trauma, chaos and challenges through which they are passing are so great that their ability to reach out for help is more limited than usual. Sometimes the circumstances can be so unique and daunting to them that clients cannot envisage how help can be given that might effectively support them. Some clients will feel threatened by the presence of a social worker, perhaps if they are guilty of a crime or are accused of harming a child or vulnerable adult.

Aggressive clients: Organisational issues

The vast majority of interactions between social workers and clients are not marked by hostility and aggression despite the challenge which social workers must sometimes present to individuals and families. Given the safeguarding tasks in which social workers often have a lead role, the effective communication that is achieved is a great tribute to the interpersonal skills of the profession.

However, incidents of aggression and violence do arise. In the United Kingdom employers have a statutory obligation to identify the nature and extent of risk (including assault) to their employees and visitors to their premises, and to devise measures to provide safe systems of work. Training and policies should cover avoiding assault, defusing aggression, breakaway techniques and – for appropriate staff – team restraint and supporting staff after an assault. As an employee you have a responsibility to undertake training and to understand and use equipment, policies and procedures. You should identify your particular training needs and communicate these through the appropriate channels through the normal mechanisms for training needs analysis.

Some social workers are employed in specialist or unusual contexts in relation to our topic. Social work in high-security prisons might be an example of this. Another example is that some social workers in Northern Ireland during the troubles have had to ensure that they are not thought to be gathering intelligence for the police despite having to collaborate with them on issues such as child protection, and have had to work within understandings worked out with proscribed paramilitary organisations for their own safety (see Chapter 5 in Darby and Williamson, 1978). In these circumstances this book must be viewed as a primer only, on which more specialist skills must be developed through training, supervision and mentoring from more experienced colleagues.

Employer support

The focus of this book is on the development of skills by beginning professionals across a range of settings. The aim is to establish a solid foundation for confident professional practice, upon which specialist skills may be built. It is important that you as a professional have support from your employer as to what represents acceptable practice in avoiding assault – to yourself, to other staff and to other clients in group care settings.

Uncertainty about employer support can lead to greater anxiety and hesitation during incidents, thereby increasing the likelihood of assault. Within your own role you should use appropriate channels to convey your concerns about any substantial perceived lack in policies, systems and arrangements to protect you from assault and aggression. It is important that you make best use of professional supervision and line management support.

After an assault it is all too common for the victim to feel that he or she is to blame in some way. Any blame for an assault must rest with the person inflicting it. If you have been assaulted or threatened in any context and reading this book raises troubling memories, do take the opportunity to seek support from an appropriate counsellor. Dealing with such issues can enable you to live life more fully yourself as well as enabling you in your helping role. Your employer probably has a contract with an employee counselling organisation which may be able to assist.

Further learning and development

This book gives you some ideas to help you to reflect on your practice and instinctive reactions to challenging situations. Reflective practice – reflecting on your practice in the light of research, theory, law, principles, policy and standards – is at the heart of professional development. For further study consider related topics such as general interpersonal skills, social work law, personal safety training and the application of therapeutic models of helping individuals, families and groups to the contexts described here.

Further research and knowledge

This text is tackling a difficult topic where little is published that is of direct help for training and supporting professionals in dealing with people who are ambivalent or aggressive. As a profession we must take every opportunity to learn and develop our professional knowledge base. This textbook may raise questions about research, evidence, theory and models for practice. Comments that might contribute to improving professional practice are welcome and should be sent to the editor at **bj.taylor@ulster.ac.uk** or care of the publishers.

Appendix

Subject benchmark for social work

Subject knowledge and understanding

5.1 During their degree studies in social work, honours graduates should acquire, critically evaluate, apply and integrate knowledge and understanding in the following five core areas of study.

5.1.1 Social work services, service users and carers, which include:

- the social processes (associated with, for example, poverty, migration, unemployment, poor health, disablement, lack of education and other sources of disadvantage) that lead to marginalisation, isolation and exclusion, and their impact on the demand for social work services;

- explanations of the links between definitional processes contributing to social differences (for example, social class, gender, ethnic differences, age, sexuality and religious belief) to the problems of inequality and differential need faced by service users;

- the nature of social work services in a diverse society (with particular reference to concepts such as prejudice, interpersonal, institutional and structural discrimination, empowerment and anti-discriminatory practices);

- the nature and validity of different definitions of, and explanations for, the characteristics and circumstances of service users and the services required by them, drawing on knowledge from research, practice experience, and from service users and carers;

- the focus on outcomes, such as promoting the well-being of young people and their families, and promoting dignity, choice and independence for adults receiving services;

- the relationship between agency policies, legal requirements and professional boundaries in shaping the nature of services provided in interdisciplinary contexts and the issues associated with working across professional boundaries and within different disciplinary groups.

5.1.2 The service delivery context, which includes:

- the changing demography and cultures of communities in which social workers will be practising;

- the complex relationships between public, social and political philosophies, policies and priorities and the organisation and practice of social work, including the contested nature of these;

- the issues and trends in modern public and social policy and their relationship to contemporary practice and service delivery in social work;

- the significance of legislative and legal frameworks and service delivery standards (including the nature of legal authority, the application of legislation in practice, statutory accountability and tensions between statute, policy and practice);

- the current range and appropriateness of statutory, voluntary and private agencies providing community-based, day-care, residential and other services and the organisational systems inherent within these;

- the significance of interrelationships with other related services, including housing, health, income maintenance and criminal justice (where not an integral social service).

5.1.3 Values and ethics, which include:

- the moral concepts of rights, responsibility, freedom, authority and power inherent in the practice of social workers as moral and statutory agents;

- the complex relationships between justice, care and control in social welfare and the practical and ethical implications of these, including roles as statutory agents and in upholding the law in respect of discrimination;

- aspects of philosophical ethics relevant to the understanding and resolution of value dilemmas and conflicts in both interpersonal and professional contexts;

- the conceptual links between codes defining ethical practice, the regulation of professional conduct and the management of potential conflicts generated by the codes held by different professional groups.

5.1.4 Social work theory, which includes:

- research-based concepts and critical explanations from social work theory and other disciplines that contribute to the knowledge base of social work, including their distinctive epistemological status and application to practice;

- the relevance of sociological perspectives to understanding societal and structural influences on human behaviour at individual, group and community levels;

- the relevance of psychological, physical and physiological perspectives to understanding personal and social development and functioning;

- social science theories explaining group and organisational behaviour, adaptation and change;

- models and methods of assessment, including factors underpinning the selection and testing of relevant information, the nature of professional judgement and the processes of risk assessment and decision-making;

- approaches and methods of intervention in a range of settings, including factors guiding the choice and evaluation of these;

- user-led perspectives;

- knowledge and critical appraisal of relevant social research and evaluation methodologies, and the evidence base for social work.

5.1.5 The nature of social work practice, which includes:

- the characteristics of practice in a range of community-based and organisational settings within statutory, voluntary and private sectors, and the factors influencing changes and developments in practice within these contexts;

- the nature and characteristics of skills associated with effective practice, both direct and indirect, with a range of service users and in a variety of settings;

- the processes that facilitate and support service user choice and independence;

- the factors and processes that facilitate effective interdisciplinary, interprofessional and interagency collaboration and partnership;

- the place of theoretical perspectives and evidence from international research in assessment and decision-making processes in social work practice;

- the integration of theoretical perspectives and evidence from international research into the design and implementation of effective social work intervention, with a wide range of service users, carers and others;

- the processes of reflection and evaluation, including familiarity with the range of approaches for evaluating service and welfare outcomes, and their significance for the development of practice and the practitioner.

5.4 Social work honours graduates should acquire and integrate skills in the following core areas.

5.5 Problem-solving skills

5.5.1 Managing problem-solving activities: honours graduates in social work should be able to plan problem-solving activities, i.e. to:

- think logically, systematically, critically and reflectively;

- apply ethical principles and practices critically in planning problem-solving activities;

- plan a sequence of actions to achieve specified objectives, making use of research, theory and other forms of evidence;

- manage processes of change, drawing on research, theory and other forms of evidence.

5.5.3 Analysis and synthesis: honours graduates in social work should be able to analyse and synthesise knowledge gathered for problem-solving purposes, i.e. to:

- assess human situations, taking into account a variety of factors (including the views of participants, theoretical concepts, research evidence, legislation and organisational policies and procedures);

- analyse information gathered, weighing competing evidence and modifying their viewpoint in light of new information, then relate this information to a particular task, situation or problem;

- consider specific factors relevant to social work practice (such as risk, rights, cultural differences and linguistic sensitivities, responsibilities to protect vulnerable individuals and legal obligations);

- assess the merits of contrasting theories, explanations, research, policies and procedures;

- synthesise knowledge and sustain reasoned argument;

- employ a critical understanding of human agency at the macro (societal), mezzo (organisational and community) and micro (inter and intrapersonal) levels;

- critically analyse and take account of the impact of inequality and discrimination in work with people in particular contexts and problem situations.

5.5.4 Intervention and evaluation: honours graduates in social work should be able to use their knowledge of a range of interventions and evaluation processes selectively to:

- build and sustain purposeful relationships with people and organisations in community-based and interprofessional contexts;

- make decisions, set goals and construct specific plans to achieve these, taking into account relevant factors including ethical guidelines;

- negotiate goals and plans with others, analysing and addressing in a creative manner human, organisational and structural impediments to change;

- implement plans through a variety of systematic processes that include working in partnership;

- undertake practice in a manner that promotes the well-being and protects the safety of all parties;

- engage effectively in conflict resolution;

- support service users to take decisions and access services, with the social worker as navigator, advocate and supporter;

- manage the complex dynamics of dependency and, in some settings, provide direct care and personal support in everyday living situations;

- meet deadlines and comply with external definitions of a task;

- plan, implement and critically review processes and outcomes;

- bring work to an effective conclusion, taking into account the implications for all involved;

- monitor situations, review processes and evaluate outcomes;

- use and evaluate methods of intervention critically and reflectively.

Communication skills

5.6 Honours graduates in social work should be able to communicate clearly, accurately and precisely (in an appropriate medium) with individuals and groups in a range of formal and informal situations, i.e. to:

- make effective contact with individuals and organisations for a range of objectives, by verbal, paper-based and electronic means;

- clarify and negotiate the purpose of such contacts and the boundaries of their involvement;

- listen actively to others, engage appropriately with the life experiences of service users, understand accurately their viewpoint and overcome personal prejudices to respond appropriately to a range of complex personal and interpersonal situations;

- use both verbal and non-verbal cues to guide interpretation;

- identify and use opportunities for purposeful and supportive communication with service users within their everyday living situations;

- follow and develop an argument and evaluate the viewpoints of, and evidence presented by, others;

- write accurately and clearly in styles adapted to the audience, purpose and context of the communication;

- use advocacy skills to promote others' rights, interests and needs;

- present conclusions verbally and on paper, in a structured form, appropriate to the audience for which these have been prepared;

- make effective preparation for, and lead meetings in a productive way;

- communicate effectively across potential barriers resulting from differences (for example, in culture, language and age).

Skills in working with others

5.7 Honours graduates in social work should be able to work effectively with others, i.e. to:

- involve users of social work services in ways that increase their resources, capacity and power to influence factors affecting their lives;

- consult actively with others, including service users and carers, who hold relevant information or expertise;

- act co-operatively with others, liaising and negotiating across differences such as organisational and professional boundaries and differences of identity or language;

- develop effective helping relationships and partnerships with other individuals, groups and organisations that facilitate change;

- act with others to increase social justice by identifying and responding to prejudice, institutional discrimination and structural inequality;

- act within a framework of multiple accountability (for example, to agencies, the public, service users, carers and others);

- challenge others when necessary, in ways that are most likely to produce positive outcomes.

Skills in personal and professional development

5.8 Honours graduates in social work should be able to:

- advance their own learning and understanding with a degree of independence;

- reflect on and modify their behaviour in the light of experience;

- identify and keep under review their own personal and professional boundaries;

- manage uncertainty, change and stress in work situations;

- handle inter- and intrapersonal conflict constructively;

- understand and manage changing situations and respond in a flexible manner;

- challenge unacceptable practices in a responsible manner;

- take responsibility for their own further and continuing acquisition and use of knowledge and skills;

- use research critically and effectively to sustain and develop their practice.

Glossary

Active aggression Entails an aggressor being actively involved in harming their target.

Affective aggression Impulsive, unplanned or thoughtless aggressive acts that arise from feelings of anger. (Also called: hostile, emotional, angry, reactive, or impulsive aggression.)

Aggression Behaviour which has as its primary aim the intention to cause harm to a target who does not wish to be harmed.

Ambivalence The emotional state of having co-existing positive and negative feelings about something or somebody.

Anger An unpleasant, universal emotion associated with bodily physiological changes and characterised by feelings of varying emotional intensity.

Direct aggression Intentionally, openly and directly attempting to cause harm to a target who does not wish to be harmed.

Indirect aggression Where the victim or target is attacked indirectly and the identity of the aggressor remains concealed.

Instrumental aggression Aggression whose primary objective is not to harm another person but to achieve another outcome which is important to the perpetrator. (Includes: incidental, cognitive, cold-blooded, or pre-meditated aggression.)

Passive aggression The intentional absence of activity by an aggressor with the primary intention to cause harm to a target.

Passive aggressive personality Chronic pattern of passively aggressive behaviour which is thought to be linked to unexpressed anger.

Postural aggression Non-verbal behaviour which does not involve physical contact between the aggressor and the target, such as threatening or intimidating facial expressions or body movements.

Resistance Unwillingness, reluctance or refusal to participate.

Resistance (psychodynamic) A client's conscious or unconscious attempts to protect themselves emotionally from interactions or events which challenge the coping mechanisms or defences they have created to manage how they feel about, or understand, their world.

References

Abbass, AA, Hancock, JT, Henderson, J and Kisely, SR (2006) Short-term psychodynamic psychotherapies for common mental disorders. *Cochrane Database of Systematic Reviews*, 4.

Ainsworth, MDS, Blehar, MC, Waters, E and Wall, S (1978) *Patterns of attachment: A psychological study of the strange situation*. Hillsdale, NJ: Earlbaum.

Allen, D (ed.) (2002) *Ethical approaches to physical interventions*. Kidderminster: British Institute of Learning Disabilities (BILD).

Anderson, CA and Bushman, BA (2002) Human aggression. *Annual Review of Psychology*, 53, 27–51.

Anderson, CA, Shibuya, A, Ihori, N, Swing, EL, Bushman, BJ, Sakamoto, A, Rothstein, HR and Saleem, M (2010) Violent video game effects on aggression, empathy, and prosocial behaviour in Eastern and Western countries. *Psychological Bulletin*, 136, 151–73.

Badlong, M, Holden, M and Mooney, A (1992) *National residential childcare project – Therapeutic crisis intervention*. Ithaca, NY: Family Life Development Centre, College of Human Ecology, Cornell University.

Bandura, A (1980) The social learning theory of aggression. In Falk, RA and Kim, SS (eds) *The war system: An interdisciplinary approach*. Boulder, CO: Westview Press.

Bandura, A, Ross, D and Ross, SA (1961) Transmission of aggression through imitation of aggressive models. *Journal of Abnormal and Social Psychology*, 63, 575–82.

Bandura, A and Walters, RH (1963) *Social learning and personality development*. New York: Holt, Rinehart & Winston Publishers.

Barrowclough, C and Tarrier, N (2000) *Families of schizophrenic patients: Cognitive behavioural intervention*. Cheltenham: Stanley Thornes.

Benson, J (2009) *Working more creatively with groups, 3rd edition*. Abingdon: Routledge.

Berkowitz, L (1989) Frustration-aggression hypothesis: Examination and reformulation. *Psychological Bulletin*, 106 (1), 59–73.

Beutler, LE, Moleiro, C and Talebi, H (2002) Resistance in psychotherapy: What conclusions are supported by research. *Psychotherapy in Practice*, 58 (2), 207–17.

Bibby, P (1994) *Personal safety for social workers*. Aldershot: Ashgate Publishing.

Bowlby, J (1988) *A secure base: Clinical applications of attachment theory*. London: Routledge.

Braithwaite, R (2001) *Managing aggression*. London: Routledge.

Brandon, M (2009) Child fatality or serious injury through maltreatment: Making sense of outcomes. *Children and Youth Services Review*, **31** (10), 1107–12.

Brazier, M, Murphy, J and Street, H (1999) *The law of torts*. London: Butterworths.

Brown, A (1994) *Groupwork*, 3rd edion. Aldershot: Ashgate.

Buss, AH (1961) *The psychology of aggression*. New York: John Wiley & Sons.

Butter-Sloss, E (1988) *Report of the inquiry into child abuse in Cleveland*. London: HMSO.

Calder, M (2003) quoted in Social Care Institute for Excellence (2005) *Managing risk and minimising mistakes in services to children and families*. London: SCIE.

Campbell, A (1993) *Men, women and aggression*. New York: Basic Books.

Campbell, JC (1995) *Assessing dangerousness: Violence by sexual offenders, batterers, and child abusers*. Thousand Oaks, CA: Sage Publications.

Carter, H, Carrell, S and Davies, C (2010) Cumbria shootings: 12 dead as gunman goes on killing spree. *The Guardian*, Thursday 3 June.

Cleaver, H and Freeman, MB (1995) *Parental persepectives in cases of suspected child abuse*. Dartington Social Research Unit. London: HMSO.

Cleaver, H, Wattam, C and Cawson, P (1998) *Assessing risk in child protection*. London: NSPCC.

Coker, AL, Davis, KE, Desai, S, Sanderson, M, Brandt, H and Smith, P (2002) Physical and mental health effects of intimate partner violence for men and women. *American Journal of Preventative Medicine*, 23 (4), 260–8.

Cooke, P (1993) TV causes violence? Says who? *The New York Times*.

Corby, B (1987) *Working with child abuse*. Milton Keynes: Open University.

Covell, NH, McCorkle, BH, Weissman, EM, Summerfelt, T and Essock, SM (2007) What's in a name? Terms preferred by service recipients. *Administration and Policy in Mental Health*, 34, 443–7.

Cramer, P (2006) *Protecting the self: Defence mechanisms in action*. New York: Guilford.

Crawford, K and Walker, J (2010) *Social work and human development*. Exeter: Learning Matters.

Darby, J and Williamson, A (eds) (1978) *Violence and the social services in Northern Ireland*. London: Heinemann Educational Books.

Department for Children, Schools and Families (2009) *Social work task force report*. London: HMSO.

Department of Health (1991) Child abuse: A study of inquiry reports 1980–1989. London: HMSO.

Department of Health (1999) *The Protection of Children Act 1999: A practical guide to the Act for all organisations working with children*. London: DoH.

Department of Health (2000) *No Secrets: Guidance on developing and implementing multi-agency policies and procedures to protect vulnerable adults from abuse*. London: HMSO.

Department of Health (2003) *Domiciliary care agencies: Minimum standards: Regulations*. London: DoH.

Department of Health (2003) *Secretary of State directions on work to tackle violence against staff or professionals who work in, or provide services to, the NHS*. London: DoH.

Department of Health (2007) *Best practice in managing risk: Principles and evidence for best practice in the assessment and management of risk to self and others in mental health services*. London: DoH.

Department of Health (2009) *Safeguarding adults: Report on the consultation on the review of No Secrets: Guidance on developing and implementing multi-agency policies and procedures to protect vulnerable adults from abuse*. London: DoH.

Department of Health and Department for Children, Schools and Families (2009) *Building a safe, confident future: The final report of the Social Work Task Fone*. London: DoH and DCSF.

Department of Health, Social Services and Public Safety (2007) Our children and young people now shared responsibility *Overflow report*, 2006. Belfast: SSI, DHSSPS.

Department of Health, Social Services and Public Safety (2008) *Family and child care. Thresholds of intervention (Understanding the needs of children in Northern Ireland)*. Belfast: DHSSPS.

Department of Health, Social Services and Public Safety (2003) *Domiciliary care agencies: Minimum standards.* Belfast: DHSSPS.

Department for Children, Schools and Families, Department of Health, Department for Work and Pensions (2008) *Raising Standards – Improving outcomes: Statutory guidance: Early years outcomes Duty: Childcare Act 2006.* London: DCSF.

Deveney, J (2010) *The impact of domestic violence on children.* Highlight 259: National Children's Board.

DHSSPS (2005) *Tackling violence at home.* Belfast: Department of Health, Social Services and Public Safety.

Dimond, B (1997) *Legal aspects of care in the community.* London: Macmillan Press.

Dobash, RE and Dobash, RP (2000) Evaluating criminal justice interventions for domestic violence. *Crime and Delinquency*, 46, 252–70.

Doel, M and Sawdon, C (1999) *The essential groupworker.* London: Jessica Kingsley.

Dollard, J, Doob, LW, Miller, NE, Maurer, OH and Sears, RR (1939) *Frustration and aggression.* New Haven: Yale University Press.

Douglas, H (2005) The development of practice theory in adult protection intervention: Insights from a recent research project. *The Journal of Adult Protection*, 7 (1), 32–45.

Douglas, T (1991) *A handbook of common groupwork problems.* London: Tavistock/Routledge.

Douglas, T (1995) *Survival in groups.* Buckingham: Open University Press.

Douglas, T (2000) *Basic groupwork*, 2nd edition. Abingdon: Routledge.

Duxbury, J and Whittington, R (2004) Causes and management of patient aggression and violence: Staff and patient perspectives. *Journal of Psychiatric and Mental Health Nursing*, 11, 172–8.

Egan, G (2002) *The skilled helper*, 7th edition. Belmont, California: Brookes Cole.

Ekman, P (2004) *Emotions revealed: Understanding faces and feelings.* Phoenix, New Jersey: Phoenix Press.

Evans, D (2001) *Emotion: The science of sentiment.* Oxford: Oxford University Press.

Eysenck, HJ (1964) *Crime and personality*. London: Methuen.

Eysenck, HJ and Gudjonsson, GH (1989) *The causes and cures of criminality*. London: Plenum Press.

Ferguson, CJ and Kilburn, J (2010) Much ado about nothing: The misestimation and over interpretation of violent video game effects in eastern and western nations. *Psychological Bulletin*, 136 (2), 174–78.

Ferguson H (2005) Working with violence: The emotions and the psycho-social dynamics of child protection: Reflections on the Victoria Climbié case. *Social Work Education*, 24 (7), 781–95.

Feshbach, S and Singer, RD (1971) *Television and aggression.* San Francisco: Jossey-Bass Publishers.

Finkelhor, D (1994) The international epidemiology of child sexual abuse. *Child Abuse and Neglect*, 18 (5), 409–17.

Fook, J (2007) Reflective practice and critical reflection. In J Lishman (ed.), *Handbook for practice learning in social work and social care.* London: Jessica Kingsley.

Ford, K, Byrt, R and Dooher, J (2010) *Preventing and reducing aggression and violence in health and social care.* Keswick: M&K Publishing.

Freedman, JL (2002) *Media violence and its effect on aggression: Assessing the scientific evidence.* Toronto: University of Toronto Press.

Freud, A (1937) (revised edition, 1968) *The ego and the mechanisms of defense.* London: Hogarth Press and Institute of Psycho-Analysis.

Freud, S (1930) *Civilization and its discontents.* London: Hogarth Press and Institute of Psycho-Analysis.

Fromm, E (1973) *The anatomy of human distructiveness.* New York: Holt, Reinhart and Winston.

Gaylard, D (2011) Policy to practice. In Mantell, A and Scragg, T (eds) *Safeguarding adults in social work.* 2nd edition. Exeter: Learning Matters.

Geen, RG (2001) *Human aggression*, 2nd edition. Buckingham: Open University Press.

Gelles, RJ (2000) Estimating the incidence and prevalence of violence against women: National data systems and sources. *Violence Against Women*, 6, 784–804.

Gilligan, J (2000) *Violence reflections on our deadliest epidemic.* London: Jessica Kingsley.

Goleman, DP (1995) Emotional intelligence: Why it can matter more than IQ for character, health and lifelong achievement. New York: Bantam Books.

Gould, N (2001) Familicide. In Howarth, G and Leaman, D (eds) *Encyclopaedia of death and dying.* London: Routledge.

Gould, N (2010) *Mental health social work.* London: Routledge.

Hague, G and Mullender, M (2006) Who listens? The voices of domestic violence survivors in service provision in the United Kingdom. *Violence Against Women*, 12, 568–87.

Harris, N, Williams, S and Bradshaw, T (2002) *Psychosocial interventions for people with schizophrenia: A practical guide for mental health workers.* Basingstoke: Palgrave Macmillan.

Hawkins, P and Shohet, R (1989) *Supervision in the helping professions: An individual, group and organizational approach.* Milton Keynes: Open University Press.

Health Service Advisory Commission of the Health and Safety Executive (1987) *Violence to staff in the health service.* London: HMSO.

Heery, G (2001) *Preventing violence in relationships.* London: Jessica Kingsley.

Heffernan, K (2006) Social work, new public management and the language of 'service user'. *British Journal of Social Work,* 36(1), 139–47.

Heider, F (1958) *The psychology of interpersonal relations.* New York: John Wiley & Sons.

Hirschi, T (1969) *Causes of delinquency.* Los Angeles: University of California Press.

Hoggett, B (1985) Legal aspects of secure provision. In Gostin, L (ed.) *Secure provision.* London: Tavistock.

Holden, M (2009) *Bringing the TCI system to your organization.* New York: Residential Child Care Project, Family Life Development Center, College of Human Ecology, Cornell University.

Horley, S (2000) *The charm syndrome.* London: Macmillan Publishers.

Howe, D (2008) *The emotionally intelligent social worker*. Basingstoke: Palgrave Macmillan.

HSE (2010a) *Evaluate the risks and decide on precautions.* London: Health and Safety Executive. **www.hse.gov.uk/risk/step3.htm**

HSE (2010b) *Violence at work.* London: Health and Safety Executive. **www.hse.gov.uk/statistics/causdis/violence/definitions.htm**

Humphreys, C and Stanley, N (2006) *Domestic violence and child protection*. London: Jessica Kingsley.

Ingleby, E (2010) *Applied psychology for social work.* 2nd edition. Exeter: Learning Matters.

Jenkins, A (2009) *Becoming ethical. A parallel, political journey with men who have abused.* Lyme Regis: Russell House Publishing.

Jones, DW (2008) *Understanding criminal behaviour: Psychosocial approaches to criminality*. Cullompton: Willan Publishing.

Keaney, F, Strang, J, Martinez-Raga, J, Spektor, D, Manning, V, Kelleher, M, Wilson-Jones, C, Wanagaratne, S and Sabater, A (2004) Does anyone care about names? How attendees at substance misuse services like to be addressed by professionals. *European Addiction Research*, 10, 75–9.

Knyazev, GG, Slobodskaya, HR and Wilson, GD (2002) Psychophysical correlates of behavioural inhibition and activation. *Journal of Personality and Individual Differences*, 33, 647–60.

Koprowska, J (2010) *Communication and interpersonal skills in social work*, 3rd edition. Exeter: Learning Matters.

Kramer, Justice Stephen (2009) R v B, C and Owens (Baby P case) Sentencing remarks, (Central Criminal Court) 22 May. **www.judiciary.gov.uk/resources**

Laevres, F (ed.) (1994) *Defining and assessing quality in early childhood education*. Leuven, Belgium: Leuven University Press.

Laming, H (2003) *Report of an inquiry*. London: The Stationery Office.

Laming, H (2009) *The protection of children in England: A progress report*. London: Stationery Office.

Lazaraus, R and Folkman, S (1984) *Stress, appraisal and coping*. New York: Springer Publishing Company.

Lindon, J (2008) *Safeguarding children and young people. Child protection 0–18 years*. London: Hodder Education.

Lindsay, I (2009) Brief solution focused therapy. In Lindsay, T (ed.) *Social work intervention*. Exeter: Learning Matters.

Lindsay, T (2005) Group learning on social work placements. *Groupwork*, 15 (1), 61–89.

Lindsay, T and Orton, S (2011) *Groupwork practice in social work.* 2nd edition. Exeter: Learning Matters.

Littlechild, B (2003) Working with aggressive and violent parents in child protection. *Social Work Practice*, 15 (1), 47–59.

Lloyd, C, King, R, Bassett, H, Sandland, S and Saviage, G (2001) Patient, client or consumer: A survey of preferred terms. *Australasian Psychiatry*, 9, 321–4.

Lorenz, K (1966) *On aggression*. London: Routledge.

Lutz, C (1988) *Unnatural emotions: Everyday sentiments on a Micronesian atoll and their challenge to western theory*. Chicago: University of Chicago Press.

Maden, T (2007) *Treating violence: A guide to risk management in mental health.* Oxford: Oxford University Press.

Madigan, L and Gamble, NC (1991) *The second rape: Society's continued betrayal of the victim.* Lexington, MA: Lexington Books.

Madoc-Jones, I and Rosco, K (2010) Women's safety service within the integrated domestic abuse programme: Perceptions of service users. *Child and Family Social Work*, 15, 155–64.

Manktelow, R (1994) *Paths to psychiatric hospitalisation: A sociological analysis.* Aldershot: Avebury.

Mantell, A and Clark, A (2011) Making choices: The Mental Capacity Act 2005. In Mantell, A and Scragg, T (eds), *Safeguarding adults in social work.* 2nd edition. Exeter: Learning Matters.

Mantell, A and Scragg, T (2011) *Safeguarding adults in social work.* 2nd edition. Exeter: Learning Mattters.

Manthorp, J, Hussein, S, Penhale, B, Perkins, N, Pinkney, L and Reid, D (2010) Managing relations in adult protection: A qualitative study of the views of social services managers in England and Wales. *Journal of Social Work Practice*, 24 (4), 363–76.

Marshall, J (2010) Family and child care: Social work practice guide. Belfast: Health and Social Care Board.

Martin, V and Henderson, E (2001) *Managing in health and social care.* London: Routledge.

Mason, T and Chandley, M (1999) *Managing violence and aggression: A manual for nurses and health care workers.* Edinburgh: Churchill Livingstone.

Mayer, JD, Salovey, P and Caruso, DR (2004) Emotional intelligence: Theory, findings, and implications. *Journal of Psychological Inquiry*, 15 (3), 197–215.

McColgan, M (2009) Task centred work. In Lindsay, T (ed.), *Social work intervention.* Exeter: Learning Matters.

McColgan, M, Campbell, A and Naylor, R, Duffy, J and Cougan, M (2006) *Childcare on the borderline: A cross-boder community audit of the useage and experience of formal and informal childcare services.* Londonderry, Northern Ireland: Derry Well Women.

McCullough, A and Parker, C (2004) Mental health inquiries, assertive outreach and compliance: Is there a relationship? In Stanley, N and Manthorpe, J (eds) *The age of the inquiry. Learning and blaming in health and social care.* London: Routledge.

McKeown, C (2008) *Facilitating social work teams in the physical disability programme of care in the Northern Health and Social Care Trust to engage service users in identifying and managing risk.* Thesis (MSc). Coleraine, Northern Ireland: University of Ulster.

McSherry, R and Warr, J (2008) *An introduction to excellence in practice development in health and social care.* Berkshire: McGraw-Hill/Open University Press.

McWilliams, M and McKiernan, J (1993) *Bringing it out into the open: Domestic violence in Northern Ireland.* Belfast: HMSO.

Merton, RK (1938) Social structure and anomie. *American Sociological Review*, 3, 672–82.

Miedzian, M (1992) *Boys will be boys.* London: Virago.

Mihalic, SW and Elliot, D (1997) A social learning theory model of marital violence. *Journal of Family Violence*, 12, 301–21.

Miller, WR and Rollnick, S (2002) *Motivational interviewing: Preparing people for change.* New York: Guilford.

Milner, J and Myers, S (2007) *Working with violence.* Basingstoke: Palgrave Macmillan.

Monahan, J, Steadman, HJ, Silver, E, Appelbaum, PS, Clark Robbins, P, Mulvey, EP, Roth, LH, Grisso, T and Banks, S (2001) *Rethinking risk assessment: The MacArthur study of mental disorder and violence.* Oxford: Oxford University Press.

Moore, DP and Jefferson, JW (2004) Passive-aggressive personality disorder. In Moore, DP and Jefferson, JW (eds), *Handbook of medical psychiatry*, 2nd ed. Philadelphia: Mosby Elsevier.

Morrison, EF (1988) Instrumentation issues in the measurement of violence in psychiatric inpatients. *Issues in Mental Health Nursing,* 9, 9–16.

Morrison, T (2001) *Staff supervision in social care.* Brighton: Pavilion Publishing.

Moss, P and Pence, A (1994) *Valuing quality in early childhood services.* London: Paul Chapman.

Mullender, A (2006) What children tell us: He said he was going to kill our mum. In Humphreys, C and Stanley, N (eds), *Domestic violence and child protection.* London: Jessica Kingsley.

Mullender, A and Morley, R (1994) Context and content of a new agenda. In Mullender, A and Morley, R (eds), *Children living with domestic violence.* London: Whiting and Birch.

Munro, E (2005) What tools do we need to improve identification of child abuse? *Child Abuse Review,* **14**, (6), 374–88.

Munro, E (2008) *Effective child protection.* Los Angeles: Sage Publications.

Munro, E (2010) *The Munro Review of Child Protection. Part One: A Systems Analysis.* Department of Education. **www.education.gov.uk/munroreview/**

Natarajan, M (ed.) (2007) *Domestic violence: The five big questions.* The International Library of Criminology, Criminal Justice and Penology. Aldershot: Ashgate.

National Confidential Inquiry into Suicide and Homicide by People with Mental Illness (2009) *Annual report.* Manchester: University of Manchester.

National Institute for Clinical Excellence (NICE) (2005*) Violence guideline.* London: NICE. **www.nice.org.uk**.

Nerenberg, L (2008) *Elder abuse prevention – Emerging trends and promising strategies.* New York: Springer.

Northern Health and Social Services Board (2006) *Safeguarding vulnerable adults.* Regional Adult Policy and Procedural Guidelines. Ballymena, Northern Ireland.

Oko, J (2010) *Understanding and using theory in social work.* 2nd edition. Exeter: Learning Matters.

Osbourne, SG and West, DJ (1979) Marriage and delinquency: A postscript. *British Journal of Criminology,* 19, 254–6.

Parrott, DJ and Giancola, PR (2007) Addressing 'the criterion problem' in the assessment of aggressive behaviour: Development of a new taxonomic system. *Journal of Aggression and Violent Behaviour,* 12 (3), 280–99.

Parton, N and O'Byrne, P (2000) *Constructive social work: Towards a new practice.* Basingstoke: Palgrave/Macmillan.

Parton, N, Thorpe, D and Wattam, C (1997) *Child protection: Risk and the moral order.* Basingstoke: Macmillan.

Paterson, B, Stark, C and Leadbetter, D (1994) Guidelines on purchasing training in the management of aggression and violence. In Multi-Sectoral Special Interest Group, *Aggression and violence management training.* Paisley, Scotland: Multi-Sectoral Special Interest Group.

Paterson, B, Turnbull, J and Aitken, I (1992) An evaluation of a training course in the short term management of aggression. *Nurse Education Today,* 12, 368–75.

147

Powis, B (2002) *Offenders' risk of serious harm: A literature review*. Research Paper 81. London: Home Office.

Pritchard, J and Kemshall, H (1995) *Good practice in risk assessment and management.* London: Jessica Kingsley.

Pugh, G (1996) *Contemporary issues in the early years*, 2nd edition. London: Paul Chapman.

Rakil, M (2006) Are men who use violence against their partners and children good enough fathers? The need for an integrated child perspective in treatment work with men. In Humphreys, C and Stanley, N (eds), *Domestic violence and child protection.* London: Jessica Kingsley.

Reader, P, Duncan, S and Gray, M (1993) *Beyond blame: Child abuse tragedies revisited*. London: Routledge.

Reid, D, Penhale, B, Manthorpe, J, Perkins, N, Pinkney, L and Hussein, S (2009) Form and function: Views from members of adult protection committees in England and Wales. *Journal of Adult Protection*, 11 (4), 20–29.

Richter, D and Whittington, R (eds) (2006) *Violence in mental health settings: Causes, consequences, management.* New York: Springer.

Ross, L (1977) The intuitive psychologist and his shortcomings: Distortions in the attribution process. In Berkowitz, L (ed.), *Advances in experimental social psychology*, 10, 173–220. New York: Academic Press.

Rowsell, C (2003) Domestic violence and children: Making a difference in a meaningful way for women and children. In Calder, MC and Hackett, S (eds), *Assessment in child care.* Dorset: Russell House Publishing.

Royal College of Psychiatrists (1998) *Management of imminent violence. Clinical practice guidelines to support mental health services.* London: Royal College of Psychiatrists.

Runciman, W (1966) *Relative deprivation and social justice: A study of attitudes to social inequality in twentieth-century England*. USA: University of California Press.

Scally, M and Lindsay, T (1997) *Teaching and assessing groupwork in a social work context.* Paper presented to the Seventh European Groupwork Symposium, Cork, July.

Schachter, S and Singer, J (1962) Cognitive, social and physiological determinants of emotional state. *Psychological Review,* 69(5), 379–99.

Schafer, J, Caetano, R and Clark, CL (1998) Rates of intimate partner violence in the United States. *American Journal of Public Health,* 88 (11), 1702–04.

Scherer, KR, Shorr, A and Johnstone, T (eds) (2001) *Appraisal processes in emotion: Theory, methods, research.* Canary, NC: Oxford University Press.

Seal, M (2008) *Not about us without us: Client involvement in supported housing.* Lyme Regis: Russell House.

Shulman, L (2009) *The skills of helping individuals, families, groups and communities.* Belmont, CA: Brooks/Cole.

Siegel, DJ (2001) Toward an interpersonal neurobiology of the developing mind: Attachment relationships, 'mindsight', and neural integration. *Infant Mental Health Journal, Special Edition on Contributions of the Decade of the Brain to Infant Psychiatry*, 22, 67–94.

Siever, LJ (2008) Neurobiology of aggression and violence. *American Journal of Psychiatry*, 165 (4), 429–42.

Simmons, L (2007) *Social care governance: A practice workbook*. Belfast: Department of Health, Social Services and Public Safety and London: Social Care Institute for Excellence.

Simon, RI and Tardiff, K (eds) (2008) *Textbook of violence assessment and management.* Washington, D.C.: American Publishing, Inc.

Skinner, EA, Steinwachs, DM and Kasper, JD (1992) Family perspectives on the service needs of families with persistent mental illness. *Innovations in Research*, 1(3), 23–30.

Smith, A (1999) Quality childcare and joint attention. *International Journal of Early Years Education*, 7(1), 85–98.

Smith, M (1975) *When I say no I feel guilty.* London: Bantam Books.

Somerset County Council and SCIE (2011) *Social care governance: A workbook based on practice in England: Workforce development SCIE guide 38.* London: Social Care Institute for Excellence.

Stanko, B (2002) *Taking stock: What do we know about interpersonal violence?* Violence Research Programme. London: Royal Holloway, University of London.

Stanley, N (2004) Women and mental health inquiries. In Stanley, N and Manthorpe, J (eds) *The age of the inquiry. Learning and blaming in health and social care.* London: Routledge.

Stanley, N and Manthorpe, J (2004) *The age of the inquiry: Learning and blaming in health and social care.* London: Routledge.

Sutherland, EH (1924) *Principles of criminology.* Chicago: University of Chicago Press.

Sylva, K, Melhuish, E, Sammons, P, Siraj-Blatchford, I and Taggart, B (2004) *The effective provision of pre-school education (EPPE) project: Intensive case studies of practice across the foundation stage.* London: DfES/Institute of Education, University of London.

Taylor BJ (2006) Risk management paradigms in health and social services for professional decision making on the long-term care of older people. *British Journal of Social Work,* 36 (8), 1411–29.

Taylor, BJ (2010) *Professional decision making in social work.* Exeter: Learning Matters.

Taylor, BJ and Devine, T (1993) *Assessing needs and planning care in social work.* Aldershot: Ashgate Publishing.

Taylor, BJ and Donnelly, M (2006) Risks to home care workers: Professional perspectives. *Health, Risk and Society*, 8 (3), 239–56.

Tuckman, BW (1965) Developmental sequence in small groups. *Psychological Bulletin,* 63, 384–99.

Turnbull, J and Paterson, B (eds) (1999) *Aggression and violence: Approaches to effective management.* Hampshire: Macmillan.

Upson, A (2004) *Violence at work: Findings from the 2002/03 British Crime Survey. Home Office Report 02/04.* London: Home Office. **www.homeoffice.gov.uk**

Varma, V (1997) *Violence in children and adolescents.* London: Jessica Kingsley.

Walby, S and Allen, J (2004) *Domestic violence, sexual assault and stalking: Findings from the British Crime Survey. Home Office Research Study 276.* London: Home Office.

Walby, S and Myhill, A (2000) *Reducing domestic violence – What works? Assessing and managing the risk of domestic violence.* London: Home Office.

Watson, D and Parsons, S (2005) *Domestic abuse of women and men in Ireland: Report on the national study of domestic abuse. NCC/ESRI.* Dublin: The Stationery Office.

Websdale, D (1999) *Understanding domestic violence.* London: Home Office.

Weisz, AN, Tolman, RM and Saunders, DG (2000) Assessing the risk of severe domestic violence: The importance of survivors' predictions. *Journal of Interpersonal Violence,* 15, 75–90.

Whitaker, DS (2001) *Using groups to help people*, 2nd edition. Hove: Brunner-Routledge.

Williams, M (1966) Limitations, fantasies and security operations of beginning group psycho-therapists. *International Journal of Group Psychotherapy*, 16, 150–62.

Willis, B and Gillett, J (2003) *Maintaining control. An introduction to the effective management of violence and aggression.* London: Arnold.

World Health Organisation (2004) *Preventing violence: An agenda to implementing the recommendations of the world report on violence and health.* Geneva: World Health Organisation.

Worral, A, Boylan, J and Roberts, D (2008) *Children's and young people's experience of domestic violence involving adults in a parenting role.* Research Briefing 25. London: Social Care Institute for Excellence (SCIE).

Index

Added to the page reference 'f' denotes a figure, 't' denotes a table and 'g' denotes the glossary.